Stress is a killer and an ine̶v̶ ... ̶e
had better learn how to de̶ ... ̶ot
overdosed with it, stress m̶ ...
helpful. Simon's book is characteristically biblical and thoughtful, and helps us to learn how to cope with stress as we see what the Bible teaches and how its subjects learned to cope. This is an excellent and helpful resource written by one who is no stranger to the issue and has, through experience, learned to cope, with a lively faith that has been tested and tried.
Wallace Benn, recently retired Bishop of Lewes and conference speaker, and his wife Lindsay Benn, speaker at women's events

For depth of biblical insight, meticulous research and a warm and personable no-guilt approach, Inter-Varsity Press is to be congratulated on bringing out this latest book by Dr Simon Vibert.
It should be required reading in colleges and seminaries on a wide scale. Further, Simon's winsome style will commend itself to all who look for personal encouragement and direction amid the stresses of today's complex society.
Richard Bewes OBE, former Rector of All Souls Church, Langham Place

Simon Vibert has written a deeply therapeutic book that goes right to the core of the problem. Stress is not so much something that *happens to us*, but something that we greatly contribute to create. It is our ambitions, our mistakes, our personality that very often keep the fire of stress burning. This is why the 'solution' to the problem is not to be found primarily outside us, but inside ourselves. From the very contents page – the titles of the twelve chapters are in themselves refreshing! – to the last page, the book is filled with practical help, a help based on wisdom that comes from personal experience, but above all from the Word of God. If you are struggling with stress, you will find soothing insights in this great little book. As a practising psychiatrist, I warmly recommend it.
Pablo Martinez, psychiatrist, author and Bible teacher

This book is a biblical 'roots, shoots and fruits' tour of stress. The Bible is full of God's leaders getting stressed at his 'stiff-necked' people. It's no surprise that today's pastors have it much the same, and so need to learn how to manage their own stress.

Yet depression is the leading cause of clergy needing time off work. Those who seek to save others often need to save themselves as well!

The Bible tells us what happens when we are out of tune with God's peace. The solution may start with getting right with God – but this book also makes it clear that a correct theology is not enough. The book's four 'companions for the journey' are all potential model church members – keen, seemingly strong, competent – yet still struggling with their emotions. In the field of mental distress, if nowhere else, theology must be applied, wrestled with and walked out.

Dr Rob Waller, Consultant Psychiatrist in Scotland and Director of Mind and Soul (www.mindandsoul.info)

Simon Vibert has produced a clear, concise introduction to the subject of stress. His focus on the biblical teaching on worry, anger, ambition, life balance, joyfulness and what it means to be a child of God all provide a helpful framework for living as our Creator intended. This, he writes, is the key to managing stress. His own story of how he has at times mismanaged stress is powerful. Throughout the book, he also provides the stories of four fictitious people, with descriptions of their lives, how they manage stress and how applying the biblical principles he identifies might help them. The similarity of these four people's lives to our own enables us to make the leap from taking what Simon writes and applying it for ourselves. All in all, this is a profoundly simple but helpful book.

Revd Ali Walton, Director of Pastoral Studies, Ridley Hall, Cambridge

It is ironic that stress-related illness seems to be on the increase, despite generally improved standards of living in recent decades. Church leaders often encounter stress in themselves and others. Simon Vibert has drawn on his own experience as a vicar and theological educator, undergoing a stressful period, to help us reach a better biblical understanding of stress and biblical approaches to coping with it. The book will be a help to those who suffer from stress and those who minister to them.

Andrew Wingfield-Digby, Vicar of St Andrew's, North Oxford, and formerly founding Director of Christians in Sport

STRESS

Simon Vibert

STRESS

The path to peace

ivp

INTER-VARSITY PRESS
Norton Street, Nottingham NG7 3HR England
Email: ivp@ivpbooks.com
Website: www.ivpbooks.com

British Library Cataloguing in Publication Data
A catalogue record for this book is available from the British Library.

ISBN: 978–1–78359–152–7

Set in Dante 12/15pt
Typeset in Great Britain by CRB Associates, Potterhanworth, Lincolnshire
Printed in Great Britain by Ashford Colour Press Ltd, Gosport, Hampshire

*Inter-Varsity Press publishes Christian books that are true to the Bible and that
communicate the gospel, develop discipleship and strengthen the church for its
mission in the world.*

*Inter-Varsity Press is closely linked with the Universities and Colleges Christian
Fellowship, a student movement connecting Christian Unions in universities and
colleges throughout Great Britain, and a member movement of the International
Fellowship of Evangelical Students. Website: www.uccf.org.uk*

This book is dedicated to my long-suffering colleagues at Wycliffe Hall, Oxford who have endured endless comments on the subject during a time of intense stress.

Thank you for bearing with me and for your many encouragements.

Acknowledgments

I am very grateful to all who have read and commented on this book: David Kratt, Jenny Tabori, Jann Eckenwiler, Vernon Rainwater, Margaret Hobbs, Richard Bewes, Stephanie Cocke, Rob Waller, Andrew Wingfield-Digby, Peter Magner, Ivor Vibert, Wallace and Lindsay Benn, and of course my marvellous IVP Editor, Eleanor Trotter. Particularly, though, I am grateful to Caroline Vibert, who has not only encouraged me through the stages of writing, but has lived and loved me through some particularly challenging times of stress, with a resolve to keep her eyes on Christ for the long haul.

Soli Deo Gloria.

Contents

Introduction: what this book is and what it is not   11

1. Stress in perspective and lessons learned   17
2. Assessing stress and remembering our Maker   26
3. Are Christians any less stressed than non-Christians?   40
4. The problem with the problem of stress   54
5. Worry and refocusing   67
6. Don't let the sun go down on your anger   80
7. Be ambitious, but for the right reasons   93
8. Work, rest and worship   108
9. Joy and thankfulness as a way of life   124
10. Relax, you are pre-approved   135
11. Let God be King   147
12. Remember that God is for you!   163

Conclusion: putting the pieces together   176

Notes   182

Introduction: what this book is and what it is not

God is not stressed. He knows the end from the beginning. All things are under his wise and sovereign control.

But the glorious world that he made is in rebellion against him. In seeking for independence from God, human beings are out of control. Control is what we most want, but we are not, and were never intended to live that way.

The conviction of this book is that it is only by realigning our desires and purposes to God's good plans that we can ultimately know relief from stress.

As an old saying goes, 'Everything will be all right in the end; if it is not all right, it is not yet the end.'

My primary interest in the topic of stress is theological, not medical, psychological or social. Although I will consider the medical definitions of stress and the physiological/ psychological implications of stress, I write as a Bible teacher and a pastor. I firmly believe that the best way to live the Christian life in this world is by working out the practical implications of good Bible teaching.

So, this is not a self-help book; there are plenty of those on the shelves of well-known high street bookshops. You may well be reading this book looking for help, and I hope that what I write will provide that. Wouldn't it be great to regain a grip of your life? Indeed it would, although I suspect that the best help comes from beyond yourself.

Our subject is a very real problem for many people today: stress and its management. In part, this is a very personal story, since, like almost everyone else, I live in a stressful world. It affects every area as I battle to live a balanced Christian life. Overwork, constant tiredness, irritability, feelings of purposelessness or the inability to achieve the things I would really like to achieve – all of these and many more are, to some extent, symptoms of stress.

Christians are not immune from these problems, and sometimes we add a few of our own into the mix as well! Thus, this book is all about you, God, and living in his twenty-first-century world.

God always seems to delight in ensuring that the lessons we learn filter through into changes in our behaviour and outlook. Recently, knowing the challenges in my life both personally and professionally during the period spent researching and writing this book, a good friend posted on my Facebook wall: 'Brother, once you have finished your book on stress, can you please think very carefully before you decide on the title of your next book?' So I can assure you that I won't be publishing anything on bankruptcy, divorce or illness . . . in the near future!

As I have researched and written this book, I have had several fictional friends in mind, although parts of all four characters are to be found in me and other people I know. These four people illustrate how certain personalities show different coping mechanisms in dealing (or not dealing) with stress. Let's think, together, how we can help them as we go along.

Thomas has more letters after his name than I have in mine. As an English teacher, he inspires his students through his engaging classes. Reading Shakespeare with him is fun. What students particularly remember, though, is his interest in them as individuals and his warm encouragement. He is also very driven. When you spend time with him, you find a certain restlessness. He is a master at getting you to talk about yourself, but, on later reflection, you will discover that you know very little about him. His mid-life crisis was serious. He bought a fancy sports car, dressed more like his sons than a middle-aged man, and his marriage began to fall apart. His family saw a side of him that no-one else saw. He fulfilled the caricature of 'a saint abroad and a devil at home'. After this, he experienced a long period of stress-induced ill health. His stress manifested itself in very subdued times of withdrawal whenever he was not at work and in highly animated, engaged attention when he was.

Susan is intimidatingly competent. She has done extremely well in her career working on a well-known national newspaper, and is supported by her husband and three young adult children. She has good negotiating skills and plans her work week like a military operation. She used to have a long drive to work, which was draining and made a huge dent in her day. Colleagues knew that the office she managed ran like clockwork when she was around. What they didn't see was how much it exhausted her, so they were surprised when she unexpectedly took sick leave. After a period off with anxiety, she negotiated a couple of days per week working from home. However, when her company went through a period of reorganization, she accepted voluntary redundancy and retrained for a less demanding career. Her family have already noticed the difference and not only are they grateful for her physical presence, but also she is more focused and relaxed when with them, and she now enjoys having her children's friends socializing with the family in the home.

In many respects, **Jack** is one of the most relaxed people I know. Others enjoy his company and feel unthreatened by his presence. He is a self-employed handyman, earning a modest wage. He is not career driven – at least, not in the way Thomas seems to be. Jack is content to earn enough money for the family and his modest hobbies. He gives the appearance of someone who is unflustered by the concerns of modern living. However, his wife Martha will testify to severe strain on their marriage relationship because of his reluctance to take responsibility, and while he appears to be in control, his lack of organization causes everyone else around him to be very stressed! In fact, Martha often feels like she has another child in the house.

Anna is a young mother, married to John. They both work: John in the financial area of the nearest city, and Anna part-time at the local primary school. Her working arrangements enable her to drop off the twins, Edward and John, at playgroup, get to work, finish work mid-afternoon, collect the twins and arrive home in time to cook dinner. Life is very full. Anna, in particular, finds the job of juggling so many balls exhausting. She feels that life consists of feeding, bathing, washing, dressing and caring for her young sons, driving them to playgroup, going to work and then returning to what seems like a never-ending treadmill of housework, cooking and bedtime. Life is so delicately balanced that it seems as though things could rapidly spin out of control if even one little thing goes wrong. Anna often finds herself musing, 'When is there time left for me or for John?'

You can see that each of these four individuals is very different. They have made various choices to get to where they are. But what is also clear is that they do not all react to life's circumstances in the same way. As we consider the impact of stress on modern Christians, we will see what each of these four people is doing right, and what they could do differently to alleviate their stress.

1. Stress in perspective and lessons learned

By any standards, 1997 was a stressful year for me. At first, I put it down to the weather. Living in Buxton, in Derbyshire's beautiful Peak District, we were used to challenging winters. When the church warden had offered me the job as vicar a few years previously, he had warned, 'Buxton has eleven months of winter and one month of bad weather.'

By March, feeling tired and a little run-down, suffering from cabin fever was not unusual. I continued to drag myself through church meetings and domestic chores, feeling like a wet weekend. So I was little prepared for the crash.

As it transpired, I had been nursing a chest infection for months. What I had put down to excessive central heating during our old folks' monthly luncheon turned out to be a raging temperature. I went to bed that Thursday afternoon. By the following day, the doctor had been called. At the weekend, I was taken by ambulance to Stepping Hill Hospital in Manchester. Pneumonia put me in hospital for a week and off work for several months.

I do believe that God uses life's circumstances to teach us Christian lessons. Ironically, I had just finished reading Philip Yancey's and Dr Paul Brand's excellent book: *Pain: The Gift Nobody Wants*.[1] Dr Brand had spent years treating leprosy sufferers. As many of you will know, leprosy is a degenerative disease causing damage to the skin, nerves and limbs. Along with this is a loss of the 'pain sensation'. Dr Brand observed that it was the accidental, self-inflicted injuries of his patients that were often the hardest to address. He had experimented with various ways to help them protect themselves from injury – for example, making them shoes so that they didn't unwittingly step on nails or glass and cut or infect their feet. But because they could not feel the sensation of a rubbing shoe and adjust accordingly, their feet became calloused or raw, and often infection resulted.

The profound point here is that pain exists for a purpose. Painlessness is debilitating; pain is actually a blessing. *Pain: The Gift Nobody Wants* is a great book with an obvious message: 'Pain is a gift from God', and I was convinced that what the authors said was true. At least, I believed it all in a theoretical way!

The day after I was admitted to hospital, the nurse asked a number of routine questions. She was surprised to learn that I was ordained. I think the main reason was a tacit assumption that, surely, as a clergyman, I didn't work hard enough to experience the physical vulnerability that was currently manifesting itself! She had obviously bought into the axiom about the clergy: 'Six days invisible; one day incomprehensible.'

In practice, the stresses faced by clergy can be intense: unsociable hours (and often working hard at times when most others are relaxing – Sunday, Christmas and Easter, for example); unrealistic expectations from those in your care (or from yourself); loneliness and isolation; lack of support; financial strain . . . The list of stresses is actually quite long. These things were all factors for me.

But added to these pressures was the fact that Carrie was expecting our third child and, as with the previous two, she was very sick throughout the whole pregnancy, enough to warrant a spell in hospital at one point. So, for me, there were domestic duties to attend to, as well as caring for our two other young children. Plus, although I was part of a loving and caring Christian family, there was a lot to do in the local and wider church. In short, I was experiencing all the symptoms of stress.

Strategies for coping

Family crises and work's demands can mix into a terribly stressful cocktail. Everyone copes in a different way. My tendency is to keep my head down, stoically fulfil my responsibilities and push myself beyond my natural reserves. The assumption is always that a quieter day is coming, that the strain will ease when I go on holiday / get an assistant / become more financially secure / the children grow up. One day.

Later, we will look at the results of some surveys that I have undertaken. To accompany one of them, I wrote a booklet entitled *Longing for Paradise*. For me, this title best encapsulates the ideological hope that keeps many of us going during times of stress. '*One day*, I'll get that dream holiday and escape from pressure.' But, as we shall see, it's not quite that simple. If we don't find ways to control and manage stress in the ordinary, everyday experiences of life, we will take them with us to our tropical island too!

Suffering is a very personal thing. We may appreciate empathy from other people, but in the end the sufferer tends to feel, 'This is my pain and it is about me', and in a very real sense, that is true. The flip side of this observation is that God uses pain and suffering to teach personal lessons to his beloved children.

There were at least three important lessons that I learned while lying on my hospital bed and subsequently through my recovery.

Lessons learned

Cope with being out of control

This might sound strange, but learning to cope with being out of control was one of the hardest lessons to learn. It was a busy period in the life of the church. Events had to be hastily cancelled when I fell ill, and other people had to stand in at short notice. I found this hard to cope with, particularly when I started to get better but still did not have much strength to play an active part in ministry.

But, to my amazement, life went on without me! Surely it is good and appropriate that church leaders should set themselves high standards. It is also good that they work hard, plan well and exercise good leadership. However, the leader is only one member of the body of Christ. Leaders should be accountable and collaborative. They should not make all the decisions in the life of the church, nor should they make the congregation overly dependent upon them.

It was not an easy lesson to learn, but it was an important one. If we feel that we carry the weight and burden of leadership on our own, we are in trouble. It is a yoke that is too hard to bear and it says more about pride in the human heart than it does about strong leadership. The best contemporary books on leadership are right to emphasize that the 'John Wayne' or 'lone-ranger' model of leadership is not always helpful. Moreover, such books concentrate on the role of the leader as coach and inspirational team leader, selling a vision and inspiring others to come on board.[2]

We are not intended to be isolated nor individualistic. This is not the same thing as saying that we are expected not to be ambitious for the kingdom of God nor to work hard (more on this later). But the growth of the kingdom of God is not dependent on me alone! The lesson I learned is in part conveyed by these wonderful words from Jesus:

> 'Come to me, all you who are weary and burdened, and
> I will give you rest. Take my yoke upon you and learn
> from me, for I am gentle and humble in heart, and you
> will find rest for your souls. For my yoke is easy and my
> burden is light.'
> (Matthew 11:28–30)

Jesus is the burden bearer, the true leader and shepherd of the people. We are given a burden, but we need to learn from him and take up a yoke that is easy and a burden that is light. Stress is reduced when we lay our burdens at the feet of Jesus and take up his easy and light burden.

Look after your body

A second important lesson for me was the need to look after my body. We are indeed 'fearfully and wonderfully made', and our bodies are described as 'temple[s] of the Holy Spirit' (Psalm 139:14; 1 Corinthians 6:19). While Jesus did warn against an excessive anxiety over food, drink and clothing (Matthew 6:25–33), it would be wrong to infer from this that our bodies do not matter. We are made in the image of God, and God's creation (while marred by sin) is indeed good (Genesis 1)! Moreover, we look forward to a day when our bodies, as well as our souls, will be redeemed (Romans 8:23; Revelation 21). We will not float around heaven in a disembodied existence.

So, we should look after our bodies because God made them. There will be times when, like the apostle Paul, we will be physically weak, sleep-deprived, cold, hungry and exposed to the elements (2 Corinthians 9), and, for the sake of devotion and discipline, we may choose to go without food, sleep or luxuries. But that is not the same thing as saying that it is inherently a sign of godliness permanently to deny ourselves the things our bodies need for healthy survival.

The analogy is often used of a rubber band. When you stretch it, it will usually return to its original shape and springiness. If you stretch it too far, it will snap. Also, if you stretch it and leave it like that for too long, it will become floppy and out of shape. So too will our bodies!

We will explore the distinction between 'good stress' and 'bad stress' in chapter 4. What is obvious is that a certain amount of adrenaline and motivation is needed in order for us to be productive. Equally obvious is the fact that we can only sustain high stress for a short period of time before we dry up, burn out or collapse. Rest is partly about sleep. But it is also about finding a rhythm for relaxation and enjoyment.

After my hospital stay, although I was slow to recognize it, I eventually realized that I had been living at full stretch for too long, and something needed to give. Many years later, I need to remember to book cardiovascular exercise into my week. (Among other benefits, it helps keep my lungs healthy.) I need to ensure, wherever possible, that I schedule a day when I am not doing my normal routine of work, keeping a 'Sabbath'. And I need to spend time enjoying God's creation and the fruit of my labour. For sure, there is an idealism articulated here, but just because it is hard to achieve does not mean that I should not keep seeking a balance in life. Stress will only be reduced if, after times of stretch and strain, the body is allowed to return to equilibrium.

Be in touch with your emotions

Physical health is one thing. But how much thought had I given to my emotional health? The third main lesson was a growing awareness of my emotional wiring or make-up. By nature, I am quite calm and stoical. But it is easy for this to slip into being impervious to circumstances.

Understanding the Myers-Briggs Type Indicator was a helpful place to start. I am an INTJ (which stands for 'introversion', 'intuition', 'thinking' and 'judgment').[3] Academics and clergy often turn out to be more introvert than extrovert, according to the Myers-Briggs test. Of course, this does not necessarily mean that they are withdrawn or unsociable. In fact, without an interest in people and good social skills, it is hard to believe that church leaders could survive in their job. This type indicator refers to the way in which you recharge your batteries and how you regain your equilibrium. For me, taking this test (several times over the years and always scoring the same result) made me realize that while I find great stimulation through being with people, I need to carve out time to be on my own, read my books, walk in the woods, or chat/pray with a close friend or my wife. Those are the things that build me up. Finding space for these things is not a selfish luxury, but rather a necessity if I am to retain emotional health. Isaiah 30:15 seems to allude to this: 'This is what the Sovereign LORD, the Holy One of Israel, says: "In repentance and rest is your salvation, in quietness and trust is your strength, but you would have none of it." '

Perfection and balance

We will return to these three things later and in particular consider how we might help Thomas, Susan, Jack and Anna. For me, the principal lesson that came out of my hospital-ization was a growing self-awareness. Jesus said, 'Be perfect, therefore, as your heavenly Father is perfect' (Matthew 5:48). He knows that he has set us an impossible ideal – he does not want us to compromise with a lesser standard. So, yes, per-fection is the goal. But generous provision is made for failures!

Similarly, we are encouraged to live a balanced Christian life, one which is in harmony with the Creator and his creation, one where we allow ourselves to be stretched for the kingdom's sake though without being burned out in the process, and one where we pay proper attention to the Lord's demand for wholeness and holiness. But this is an ideal that we keep working towards. Balance in this life is unattainable, but never-theless it is the goal to motivate us. I am not suggesting an isolated monastic existence. In fact, the reason why this rhythm of life is so important is because it actually makes us more productive. How often have I been reading, writing and thinking hard at my desk but unable to 'think myself clear'. Then, in a twenty-minute walk around the wonderful University Parks (right next to my office), it all falls into place. The clarity found in the park would not happen without the slog at the desk. But, I also believe, the time at the desk will often not produce the clarity needed without the break to allow mind and body to refresh themselves.

My left lung continues to carry some damage. It is my weak spot. Paul had a 'thorn in the flesh'. Some think that it may have been an ophthalmic problem (suggested by Galatians 6:11). But actually, we don't know. What we do know is that pain and frustration dogged him throughout his life. He pleaded for the 'thorn' to be removed. But he heard from the Lord that it was better that it remained: 'My grace is sufficient for you, for my power is made perfect in weakness' (2 Corinthians 12:9). Indeed, Paul was able to boast in his weaknesses because it was this that made him humble, dependent and better enabled for the Lord to work through him.

In this chapter, I have shared my personal story. You will have your own 'thorn in the flesh', that area of weakness that will manifest itself when you are most vulnerable. As we continue to explore how to live a Christian life in a stressful world, we will need to remember that dealing with stress is very personal to you. We all need to grow in self-awareness. And God will continue to work through the circumstances in which we find ourselves in order to shape us into the likeness of Christ and use us in his service. My experience is my own. But I believe that the pressures from stress and the lessons learned are not unique.

We should take some comfort from the fact that we are not alone in experiencing stress, and while the way we label it might have changed, stress is not a twenty-first-century disease. This could also mean that the remedy might just be simpler than we sometimes imagine.

2. Assessing stress and remembering our Maker

Growing up in the Channel Islands, in Jersey, the sea was my constant companion and the best stress-buster I knew. My childhood was spent on the beach. Even as a young adult, I would spend as much time as I could on the sea (sailing), in the sea (swimming) or by the sea (fishing). I would always know the state of the tide and its ebb and flow.

But this was more than just leisure. The sea provided, and provides, me with a sense of the vastness of God's created world. It produces a feeling of awe and wonder, particularly as I watch the tide racing up the beach or view waves crashing over the rocks. The vast ocean engenders respect.

The tidal flow in Jersey is huge – on a spring tide, the sea will rise up to forty vertical feet, progressing several miles up the beach. Consequently, there are warnings at the top of every slipway which read: 'Time and Tide wait for no man.' After a while, it became easier to walk past those warning signs without taking in the urgency of the message. One of my friends discovered the truth of it to his cost, when he nearly lost his life after getting distracted in the rock pools along the low-tide mark. He was only rescued from a remote sandbank because someone heard his cries and called the lifeboat.

The symptoms of stress are warning signs too. They remind us that we are mortal; our bodies' needs must be attended to.

For many people, the sight of the sea is a great stress-buster. Most of us crave contact with the natural world as a means of getting our troubles back into perspective.

A modern disease?

A conversation with the average urban professional in the twenty-first century might lead you to conclude that stress is a constant companion from which there is little escape. What I think this chapter will reveal is that stress is not new, and also that it is not necessarily linked to geography, gender or career. Having said that, I think it is not without significance that a recent poll names Hawaii as the least-stressed American state! Sun-kissed beaches, deep blue sea and tropical landscapes seem the perfect escape from noisy urban living. Nevertheless, stress is as much about a person's outlook on life as it is about external pressure and circumstances. Alleviating stress, in part, involves acknowledging our personality differences and coming to understand our own triggers.

In 2005, Hoegaarden Beers published the results of a survey of 2,000 adults that had asked questions about their experience of stress and the main ways in which they found relief. It concentrated on the understandably high levels of stress experienced by city dwellers, many of whom worked long hours with very little contact with the natural world.[1]

According to this survey, across the UK, 30% of the entire population claimed to experience daily stress. Clearly, urban living was a major contributory factor, as this figure reduced to 19% for country dwellers. Key stresses were: the daily commute to work; urban noise; the lack of sight of wildlife; work itself; or even just getting out of bed! The survey commented that many city dwellers could spend up to seventy-three days without more than five minutes of silence at a time. Hence there is an increasing tendency to create compact urban gardens and park spaces in city centres. This, historically, was one of the motivating factors behind Ebenezer Howard's commitment to Letchworth and Welwyn Garden City.[2]

Those surveyed by Hoegaarden Beers indicated that the best stress-buster was to be in contact with nature. Indeed, 84% indicated that this helped reduce stress. Others said that good stress relief was to be found in:

- the sight of the sea (42%)
- a walk in the park (33%)
- hearing birds singing (14%)
- smelling freshly cut grass (10%).

Urbanization, instant communication and noise pollution are all significant factors in elevating stress. However, as we have noted, stress is not a twenty-first-century problem, nor is it limited to the inner city. Moreover, I think we are also agreed that changing our environment is not in itself sufficient to change our attitudes and reactions to pressures and worries.

I think that most people would acknowledge that we need help more generally in our globally connected modern culture which seems never to sleep, a world which has seemingly 'shrunk' and is constantly interconnected through modern technology. We see fantastic electronic advances, yet nevertheless struggle with the reality of living with any sense of equilibrium.

Human beings are created by a good God who 'richly provides us with everything for our enjoyment' (1 Timothy 6:17). Paul contrasts God's provision with the tendency of wealth to focus our attention on the present world, instil pride in us and entice us to look to money as our source of happiness. We also remember that God wants human beings to delight in the world that he has made – just as he did: 'He saw that it was good' (Genesis 1:10, 12, 18, 21, 25); 'The heavens declare the glory of God' (Psalm 19:1); 'the earth is the LORD's, and everything in it . . .' (Psalm 24:1). Hence, 'I lift up my eyes to the mountains – where does my help come from? My help comes from the LORD, the Maker of heaven and earth' (Psalm 121:1–2).

The responses articulated in the Hoegaarden Beers survey are hardly surprising when one considers the emphasis placed on the need for human beings to stay connected with the God who made this good world.

Yet stress is difficult to measure, for two reasons. Firstly, defining what constitutes stress is complex. (This will be the focus of the following chapters.) Secondly, and related to the difficulty of definition, is the fact that the experience of stress is very subjective and no two people will react to potentially stressful situations in the same way. I can think of a friend for whom the sound of a crying baby, someone's mobile phone conversation in the quiet carriage of the train or a barking dog is enough to get him huffing and puffing and muttering under his breath. Yet this same friend seems to get through a day negotiating multinational contracts worth millions of pounds without even breaking into a sweat. Clearly, his comfort zone is different from mine!

Despite the complexities, there are those who have attempted a less subjective assessment of stress.

Stress plus

Back in 1967, psychiatrists Thomas Holmes and Richard Rahe contacted more than 5,000 patients over a two-year period in order to discover whether stress contributed to major illness.[3] The results of this extensive survey still resonate decades later. The reason for their abiding significance is that Holmes and Rahe attempted a more objective approach to the study of stress, with some evidence that they might be able to predict its implications.

They identified forty-three life events (or 'Life-Change Units') and asked contributors to score them according to whether they had had recent experience of them. The higher the score, the higher the stress.

This self-test is assumed to give an indication of the likelihood of illness or accident according to the amount of prolonged stress experienced by the individual. Holmes and Rahe argued that if the Life-Change Units, when added together, scored below 150, there was a 35% chance of illness or accident within two years. If, however, the LCU totalled between 150 and 300, there was a 51% chance, and for a LCU combined score over 300, there was an 80% chance of illness or accident.

Although there is still a large amount of subjectivity in this method of scoring, Holmes and Rahe argue that the large sampling of people gives a strong indication of how much stress is likely to be induced by these various events.

By comparing a control group of people who had 'normal' stress levels with patients who had scored highly on the Life-Change Units scale, Holmes and Rahe demonstrated a link between high stress and illness. So it would be wise to infer that where it is possible to reduce the environments that cause stress, you will be more likely to reduce the chances of the onset of illness.

Holmes and Rahe Life-Change Scale Stress Test
(summary of key stresses)[4]

Life event	Event value
1. Death of spouse	100
2. Divorce	73
3. Marital separation	65
4. Jail term	63
5. Death of close family member	63
6. Major personal injury/illness	53
7. Marriage	50
8. Being fired from work	47
9. Marital reconciliation	45
10. Retirement	45
11. Major change in family member's health	44
12. Pregnancy	40
13. Sex difficulties	39
14. Addition to family	39
15. Major business readjustment	39
16. Major change in financial status	38
17. Death of a close friend	37
18. Change to a different line of work	36
19. Major change in number of marital arguments	35
20. Taking on a mortgage	31
21. Foreclosure of mortgage/loan	30
22. Major change in work responsibilities	29
23. Son/daughter leaving home	29
24. Trouble with in-laws	29

Life event	Event value
25. Outstanding personal achievement	28
26. Spouse beginning or ceasing work	26
27. Starting or finishing formal schooling	26
28. Major change in living conditions	25
29. Revision of personal habits	24
30. Trouble with the boss	23
31. Major change in work hours, conditions	20
32. Change in residence	20
33. Change in school	20
34. Major change in usual type and/or amount of recreation	19
35. Major change in church activity	19
36. Major change in social activities	18
37. Taking out a loan	17
38. Major change in sleeping habits	16
39. Major change in number of family get-togethers	15
40. Major change in eating habits	15
41. Vacation	13
42. Celebrating Christmas/Hanukkah/other major holidays	12
43. Minor violation of law	11

It appears fairly universally agreed that the score from the Holmes and Rahe Stress Test (of which the result is called the Social Readjustment Rating Scale) sets the standard for assessing the amount of stress in a person's life and the likelihood of it causing a long-term impact. So, not only does stress need to be taken very seriously, but there is some evidence for the belief that the health impact of high stress will be felt within a year or two.

It might be worth pausing for a moment to work out your score.[5] The fact that you have picked up this book may already be a good indication of your stress level. I was perversely encouraged by my score insofar that it helped me to appreciate the confluence of factors causing stress. I also took it as a warning of the potential impact. A simpler (and less scientific) test appears on the BBC website, based on research by the British Association for Counselling and Psychotherapy undertaken for the 2013 National Stress Awareness Day. I confess to being relieved that I just came in the 'low-stress' category (despite the rush to finish this book!).[6]

Bible help

In May 2013, after ten years of absence, best-selling singer/ songwriter Amy Grant announced her new album, *How Mercy Looks From Here*. Reflecting on the impact of something that her mother had said to her prior to her death in 2011, Amy shared the following:

> At some point in life you realize that some things really matter and some things don't. Living matters. Celebrating life matters. Seeing the value in hard times matters. Relationships and people matter. Faith matters. I feel like that's where my head has been while writing and recording this project. I feel this is a very positive record. I hope it is life affirming. Life prepares us for the journey. You don't know what's ahead and that is one of the great things about getting older in a framework of faith. Faith is the one thing that stands the test of time.[7]

It would seem that, for Amy Grant, arriving at a point where she can be creative and make music again has required living through some difficult experiences and making sense of them with God in the picture. Her score on the Holmes and Rahe scale would be high, particularly bearing in mind her divorce from Gary Chapman. Her quote is particularly interesting because the reflections on her life experience allude to, but do not mention by name, the stress which keeps us from being the people we believe we were created to be.

As we have seen, at one level, stress is not new. It has been around as long as human beings have wrestled with the disconnection between what they strive to do and how they plan to live and the reality of their present experiences.

Many of the Psalms wrestle with this feeling of disconnection, for example, Psalm 25:

In you, LORD my God,
  I put my trust.

I trust in you;
    do not let me be put to shame,
    nor let my enemies triumph over me.
No one who hopes in you
    will ever be put to shame,
but shame will come on those
    who are treacherous without cause.

Show me your ways, LORD,
    teach me your paths.
Guide me in your truth and teach me,
    for you are God my Saviour,
    and my hope is in you all day long.

Remember, LORD, your great mercy and love,
 for they are from of old.
Do not remember the sins of my youth
 and my rebellious ways;
according to your love remember me,
 for you, LORD, are good.

Good and upright is the LORD;
 therefore he instructs sinners in his ways.
He guides the humble in what is right
 and teaches them his way.
All the ways of the LORD are loving and faithful
 toward those who keep the demands of his covenant.
For the sake of your name, LORD,
 forgive my iniquity, though it is great.

Who, then, are those who fear the LORD?
 He will instruct them in the ways they should choose.
They will spend their days in prosperity,
 and their descendants will inherit the land.
The LORD confides in those who fear him;
 he makes his covenant known to them.
My eyes are ever on the LORD,
 for only he will release my feet from the snare.

Turn to me and be gracious to me,
 for I am lonely and afflicted.
Relieve the troubles of my heart
 and free me from my anguish.
Look on my affliction and my distress
 and take away all my sins.
See how numerous are my enemies
 and how fiercely they hate me!

> Guard my life and rescue me;
>> do not let me be put to shame,
>> for I take refuge in you.
> May integrity and uprightness protect me,
>> because my hope, LORD, is in you.

> Deliver Israel, O God,
>> from all their troubles!

David does not speak specifically of stress here. However, he describes life circumstances that, if articulated in modern parlance, would most probably fall into the category of stress.

David puts his confidence, hope and trust in God, even when other people or circumstances intend rather to put him to shame (vv. 1–3).

He wants direction for his life and sincerely desires to follow God's true ways, but his failure and guilt weigh him down, and hence he asks for mercy and asks that God, out of his goodness, would not remember his sin (vv. 4–7).

He seeks active guidance from God and instruction in his ways, confident that God will confide in those who fear him (vv. 8–15).

The psalmist appeals to God that he might come close because the burdens of life weigh heavily upon him. He experiences internal turmoil: loneliness, affliction, trouble in heart and anguish. He cries for deliverance from sin (vv. 15–19) and the removal of shame and trouble (vv. 20, 22).

As well as inner turmoil, there are external threats to his peace by 'enemies', from whom he asks for deliverance (v. 22).

His overall desire is for integrity and uprightness, that is, a character that is honouring to God and that enables him to live his life with pure motives despite challenging circumstances (v. 21).

In short, the psalmist seems very aware of the apparently modern phenomenon of stress.

The following phrases are taken from responses given to my personal surveys, which you will learn more about in the next chapter. Note the remarkable resonance with Psalm 25:

- 'feeling anxious about things'
- 'feeling out of control'
- 'having more to do than the time available'
- 'experiencing physical symptoms of stress'
- 'wanting space for recovery after a period of intense activity'.

Stress is part of the fallen human condition, and it seems, this has always been the case.

However, at another level, although stress is not new, it is named today as a dominant feature of contemporary living. Whatever walk of life one comes from, stress seems endemic. As we have already noted, ours is a globally connected, shrinking and insomniac age, enjoying the enormous benefits of modern technology, but not seeming to know how to find rest or any sense of equilibrium. These, indeed, are new challenges for us.

Conclusion

Biblical wisdom refocuses our attention off the real, but temporary, challenges of living in this world. Rather, our gaze should be upon the God who made us. He is the same Lord who made this world and knows us through and through. Though the created order is flawed and marred by sin at every level, if we make the time and have the eyes to see, we will discern God's good hand in all that he has made.

Spending time by the sea, in the countryside or in the hills should cause us to marvel at God's power and goodness. This helps us to put our trials and difficulties in perspective. Time in the created world should give us confidence that, if the Lord can sustain this earth and recreate each new day, he is more than big enough to deal with the details of our everyday lives.

The part of the Bible known as the wisdom writings offers practical and pithy advice for us today. For example, Ecclesiastes seems to acknowledge that it is easy to slip into a cynical and negative attitude, particularly when we are beaten down by the pressures of daily living. Therefore, the writer counsels,

Remember your Creator
    in the days of your youth,
before the days of trouble come
    and the years approach when you will say,
      'I find no pleasure in them.'
(Ecclesiastes 12:1)

We will now circle back to the four characters whom I mentioned in the introduction. In fact, most chapters will have a message for one or more of them.

 Getting personal

Thomas is a competent academic with a messy personal life. I suggest that part of the issue is that he needs to find a way to relax. He does not know what to do with himself when he is not busy, and he has spent most of his adult life finding his identity in his work (apart from his mid-life

crisis, of course). He does not always need to be in control. Spending time in God's world, marvelling at the Creator, slowing his racing heart – all of these things will help alleviate Thomas's stress.

Anna too will need to find space to enjoy the moment. Her day is full of looking after lively twins or preparing for lessons to teach or juggling the busyness of the household. She starts sentences with: 'It will be easier when the children are older . . .' or 'It will be easier when we earn a little more money . . .' It is tempting always to think 'one day . . .' and to live for the next holiday, for when the children go to school, go to university or leave home, or when we retire. But instead of rushing from work to collect the children from playgroup, Anna could walk across the park once a week instead of driving. Or, perhaps, in that short breathing space between dropping off the kids and walking into work, she could park the car and read a psalm and briefly pray.

Think of a 'Thomas' or an 'Anna' whom you need to encourage to focus on the One who controls everything.

3. Are Christians any less stressed than non-Christians?

From 1998 to 2007, I was the vicar of a church in Wimbledon. The parish was largely composed of young professionals, attracted by a leafy part of London yet able to make the relatively short commute into the centre of the city. Most were married with pre-school-aged children. In fact, for a time, this part of Wimbledon boasted the highest birth-rate per head of population in Europe. The small, expensive, terraced houses were great first homes for newlywed couples, but too small for larger families. The results from the surveys mentioned in the last chapter resonate well with my own experience as a church pastor in Wimbledon.

Congregation members would frequently cite stress as being a common reason why they felt unable to relax or unable to be fully engaged in some aspects of the life of the church. They spoke about stress as a major contributory factor in tiredness, headaches, back pain and other physical complaints. They also indicated that they wanted relief from stress but did not necessarily know how to achieve it in the short term. Stress relief was to be found in the next holiday, or when the children left home, or perhaps when retirement plans came to fruition. It all seemed rather elusive.

If I was to provide pastoral support to my congregation, I needed to establish how widespread these feelings of stress were. So, I and my colleagues started talking with people in the parish, because we found that by asking them about stress, we had a natural avenue into the local community. Interestingly, their experience of stress was very similar to that experienced by members of my congregation.

Stress in the city?

But how exactly do you engage busy young professionals in conversations about the Christian faith? Leafleting is not very productive; it merely fills their porch with recyclable material (along with takeaway menus and offers for cheap loft extensions). Door-to-door conversation – once the mainstay of parish evangelism – can be problematic, not least because of the homeowner's assumption that they will answer the door to a 'religious nutter' or a member of a sect who will engage in a 'heavy sell'. And, after all, following a hot and tiring commute, most homeowners want to retreat to their living rooms and not be pestered on the doorstep. For many, 'an Englishman's home is his castle', and the draw-bridge is raised at the end of a working day. You cross over at your own peril!

Our church was well aware of these pressures. However, we did not stay away. On the contrary, over a two-week period in the early summer of 2001, we succeeded in talking with several hundred individuals about the Christian faith on the doorsteps of their own homes. And the strategy we adopted did seem to achieve genuine engagement with members of our parish.

Firstly, we introduced ourselves as members of the local church, 'just down the road', with a spire clearly visible between them and the London underground station. That helped: we were in the community and for the community.

Secondly, we said, 'We are here to conduct a very short survey on the subject of stress.' This almost always elicited responses along the lines of: 'Ah! Tell me about stress . . . you would not believe my day . . .'

Thirdly, following the simple questions outlined below, we made two offers: we invited them to take *Longing for Paradise*, the booklet I had written to accompany our visiting, and we also invited them to join an Alpha course, which would run a few months later.[1] Incidentally, at this Alpha course we would have the highest participation rate ever, with fifty attendees.

We received seventy-five responses to the survey from within the church congregation. We received 182 from door-to-door visiting, not to mention the many more conversations with people who were 'too stressed to complete the survey'!

Once all the results had been collated, I sent a glossy sheet with the results to all 1,500 homes in the parish. The questions and results of the survey were summarized as follows:

View from the doorstep

Question 1: 'How often do you experience stress?'
    Parish: 5% never; 31% occasionally; 6% monthly;
    26% weekly; 32% daily.
    Congregation: 1% never; 33% occasionally; 4% monthly;
    16% weekly; 46% daily.

In the light of the above, it would appear that church attendance does little to reduce stress. In fact, it might even be that the focus on heaven and eternity raises extra tensions. Conclusion? Don't come to church for an easy life! If you think that church is made up of tambourine-waving, sandal-clad semi-nomads, well, this survey would seem to indicate that Christians really do live in the same world as everyone else!

Question 2: 'Do you think that the Christian faith offers help with stress?'

Parish: 11% no; 19% not sure; 70% yes.

Congregation: 3% no; 9% not sure; 88% yes.

Obviously, this was a very subjective question. Some respondents may well have answered it according to how they perceive people with a committed Christian faith would have responded. However, it does seem that the Christian faith helps put this life in its proper perspective and might in fact offer the 'peace which transcends all understanding' (Philippians 4:7) promised to Jesus' followers.

Question 3: 'Do you think that the Christian faith offers real hope for life beyond the grave?'

Parish: 16% no; 30% not sure; 54% yes.

Congregation: 1% no; 18% not sure; 81% yes.

The remarkable thing is that although national church attendance is nowhere near that high, 54% of respondents appear to retain some kind of hope in life beyond the grave. It is the conviction of the local church that the afterlife is not 'pie in the sky' when you die, but rather that hope is the privilege of those who have come to follow Jesus Christ as Rescuer and King. If 81% of church attendees have this assurance, might this be a compelling case for investigating the faith further?

The doorstep conversations and follow-up leaflet enabled the exchange to move naturally from felt need ('I am stressed') to real need: peace with and from God. The peace which passes understanding will guard hearts and minds in the knowledge and love of God (Philippians 4:7). Such peace first comes through acknowledging the lordship of Christ and humbly repenting of sin, leading on to a solid confidence in God for now and for the future.

Focus on 'Christian' stress

Over a decade later, in 2013, I undertook two similar surveys. They were:

- questions sent to Wycliffe Hall staff and students, primarily Christians (resulting in sixty-eight responses)
- Survey Monkey Facebook friends/personal contacts, a mixture of Christian and non-Christian friends (resulting in fifty-nine responses).

Out of 140 people surveyed in 2013 at Wycliffe, half of the respondents were students in the twenty-five to forty age group. The Facebook survey over the same period had a higher average age: closer to fifty.

The results of the combined surveys were as follows.

Question 1: 'How often do you experience stress?'

- Never 0%
- Occasionally 44%
- Monthly 2%
- Weekly 32%
- Daily 22%

Comments from participants: 'Whether I feel stress? It depends on how it is defined'; causes of stress: 'feelings of helplessness . . . culminations of several events all happening at once'.

Question 2: 'What is the number-one tell-tale sign that you are stressed?'

- Irritability 39%
- Sleep trouble 30%
- Withdrawal 12%
- Fear 10%
- Overeating/undereating 3%
- Other 6%

Comments from participants: Several people said that there was no number-one sign; a combination of all the above occurred. Other tell-tale signs: 'skin conditions', 'stomach complaints', 'headaches', 'muscle tensions', 'tightening around the heart', 'paralysis', 'grumpy, snappy, anxious [feelings]', 'inability to think straight', 'escapism', 'nightmares'.

Question 3: 'Does the Christian faith offer help with your stress? Why/why not?'

- Yes 94%
- No 6%

Comments from participants (summarized)
God is our Father: 'We have the perspective of a sovereign Father . . . I am not at the centre . . . Faith gives perspective'; 'I am noticed by someone when I am stressed.'

God is in control: 'God has it all under control, even if I don't. This is by far the greatest help whenever I am stressed.'

God answers prayer: 'Prayer helps me lift my concerns to God . . . reminds me of the bigger picture . . . "relativizes" the problem'; 'Praying through gritted teeth in stressful moments often [results in] experiencing grace / patience / strength . . .'; 'I cast my anxieties on God' (1 Peter 5:6–7).

The Bible is my rule and guide: 'The Bible reveals how we should be humble before God when faced with anxieties'; 'Faith assists in calibrating my attitude'; 'Focusing on Christ instead of on self'; 'God's Word helps me order my day'; 'Meditating on Bible passages such as "well done good and faithful servant" and Matthew 6:25–34 helps to reduce stress'; 'Prayer and Scripture help, but sometimes this exacerbates the stress by making me think too much about others . . . and this can pile on the guilt'; 'Church is often the cause of stress.'

God gives his Holy Spirit: 'True peace, the fruit of the Spirit' (Philippians 4:6–7).

Question 4: 'What are the three main ways in which you deal with stress? (E.g. what do you do, what do you 'tell yourself' and how do you get help?)

Popular answers included prayer, exercise and self-discipline (especially combined into 'a good rhythm of sleep, food, exercise'). Some cited distractions, such as praising, listening to music, or drinking wine (in moderation, of course!). Other things that helped were: talking things over with a spouse or friend; reminding yourself that you are loved; reprioritizing; allowing the gospel to put stress in perspective; physical touch from a spouse; verbalizing / naming frustration; writing lists; reducing workload if possible; gritting your teeth and getting on with it; and moving away from noise and into nature.

Several people also noted that the issue was not primarily about knowing the answers, but rather, when highly stressed, it was about finding the time and the will to put solutions into practice. In this context, other issues surfaced in this response relating to problems of procrastination, escapism and denial, obsessiveness and the overuse of alcohol/food to alleviate symptoms. There is a clear discrepancy between knowing the right answers and the will/ability to break the cycle and get around to doing things that will help.

What can we learn?

Intriguingly, there was little difference in the responses or comments from both surveys regarding the impact of stress. I also noted that in terms of gender balance (40% of responses were female), younger female responses indicated similar stress levels to those of their male counterparts, whereas among the older group, the men spoke of more stress than the women. This may be reflective of changing career choices/ gender roles over time, or it might simply be that the younger group was almost all composed of students (of both sexes) experiencing similar study stresses and preparing for similar pastoral roles. A more discrete comparison of stress experiences across the genders would be worth undertaking.

The limitations of my surveys are similar to those of the Hoegaarden one, namely that the responses are subjective (unlike the Holmes and Rahe Stress Scale, which attempts some more objective criteria). However, the subjectivity was also intentional. In order to help Christians deal with stress today, I need to be able to understand their experience of stress and how they intuitively react to it.

I made a number of other observations. From both of the 2013 surveys, I found the most interesting thing was that while both believers and non-believers experienced stress, the way in which the two groups addressed and alleviated it seemed to be different. Christians should not despair! We have rich resources available to help us deal with stress. The gospel offers peace with God, neighbour and self, and really does help put life's troubles into proper perspective.

There is some mild, albeit perhaps perverse, encouragement in realizing that if you undergo stress, you are not alone. While there were a few people who denied experiencing stress at all, they were a distinct minority. There is evidence to suggest that younger people (those between 18 and 30) experience more stress than their older counterparts.[2] However, it has been wisely observed that what we label as stress today, others in the early part of the twentieth century might have called 'depression' or 'anxiety'. Literature from the Middle Ages refers to other more pressing ailments such as consumption, influenza and cholera, which resulted in a much shorter lifespan, and at one level, the stresses of life were related to surviving in a totally different medical, social and cultural climate.

In reality, the kinds of stresses from my surveys have been exacerbated by things electronic. We have already seen how constant interconnectivity through email, smartphones and social networking means that we find it harder to switch off – literally! We have ambitious expectations of doing it all, which in turn cause us to be overwhelmed by a sense of endless opportunity and expectation. These aspects of modern living often mean that we do not allow ourselves the necessary recuperation or downtime. Alongside these factors are the pace of life, the expectations of travel, and the associated noise and pollution that result. All these things are part of the background drone noise which can gnaw away at us. For these and many more reasons, we are right to conclude that previous generations did not experience stress in quite the same way as we do now.

Reordering our world around Christian principles

Here are three principles that arise as a result of observations from my surveys. We will look at each of them in more detail later.

1. Work is good but overwork is not

Work is a privilege and a gift from God. But 'work' became 'toil' after our forebears disobeyed God and were thrown out of the garden (Genesis 1 – 3). Work-related stress is often caused by the sense of having more to do than can realistically be achieved, through lack of planning and organization or through other factors imposed upon us from the outside, like a demanding boss or pressing deadlines. As many unemployed people will testify, we do want to work. However, overwork needs to be managed well.

In order to write this book, I have had to clear my diary, refrain from emailing and social media, and focus my attention in a concentrated way. There is some satisfaction in this kind of work. But I am also very aware of what I am leaving undone – it is often in the back of my mind – and I am also conscious that I am rather good at self-interruption, whether that be pouring myself another cup of coffee or indulging in a quick surf of the internet.

I need to remind myself that there were good things that even the Lord Jesus chose *not to do*. For example, in Mark chapter 1, Jesus healed Simon Peter's mother-in-law, and large crowds arrived after sunset on the Sabbath day. Jesus would have been very late in getting to bed that night. Early the next day, the crowds were lining up at the front door clamouring for Jesus' attention. When Simon Peter emerges a little while later, he searches for Jesus, discovers that he had left the house before dawn, and eventually finds him praying. It is not without a degree of exasperation that Simon Peter says to him, 'Everyone is looking for you' (v. 37). Jesus replies that they will move on elsewhere in order for him to prioritize preaching. I have often pondered what little effort it would have taken the Son of God to heal all the people at Peter's door. A word? A touch? But in order to emphasize the preaching of the gospel, he chose not to return to the house. Praying to his Father realigned his priorities. (Notice the same pattern in Gethsemane before going to the cross in Mark 14:32–40.)

As I hacked my way around the golf course with a friend recently, he said to me, 'It is important that I do something in life that means that I think of nothing else while I am doing it.' Good advice! For some, it is golf (although I confess that my poor performance on the course does not always guarantee a complete escape from feeling stressed). Some people will find this break from the pressures of work through other sports or music or time with friends.

2. Prayer, peace and God's presence are a great comfort

Related to this point, the surveys strongly suggest that, for Christians, prayer is the place where we gain God's perspective and ascertain his priorities. There are countless explicit and implicit ways in which Christians are encouraged to bring their anxieties and stresses to God. For example, in the Lord's Prayer, Jesus teaches us to pray for *daily* bread, for his will to be done on earth, and that we would trust our Father in heaven.[3] The regular repetition of this form prayer reminds us of our utter dependence on God.

Dependence on God's faithful character is also implied in the truth of Romans 8:28: 'We know that in all things God works for the good of those who love him, who have been called according to his purpose.' It would be wrong to interpret this verse in a way that is simplistic or trite; it is not a fortune-cookie promise. The truth of this text needs some unpacking and careful application. (We will do this in chapter 11.) However, it should give us great confidence that even through difficult and trying circumstances, God is working for our benefit, even if that might not be immediately obvious to us.

Christians are united in believing that through prayer we realign ourselves to God's purposes for our lives. And as we do so, we benefit from God's presence in our stress, enabling us to draw help from this verse which we have already quoted:

Do not be anxious about anything, but in every situation, by prayer and petition, with thanksgiving, present your requests to God. And the peace of God, which transcends all understanding, will guard your hearts and your minds in Christ Jesus.
(Philippians 4:6–7)

We will need to spend some more time thinking through the kind of prayer that will ensure that God is centre-stage in our lives.

3. The Bible is a rich resource of promises about God

Many of the responses revealed that Christians rely heavily upon God's Word as sustenance and nourishment during times of stress. The Bible is authored by God, through human personalities who spoke their words and God's words.

Christians can know God through the Bible, but alongside that, as John Calvin memorably wrote, Christians also come truly to know themselves.[4]

The Bible not only provides rich wisdom to help us live for God in this world and prepare for life in the next, but also it is a mirror by which we see ourselves as both created and loved by the Father, but at the same time frail and fallen human beings. We will spend some time later thinking about the Bible's diagnosis and potential cure for stress.

You will be aware that I have not yet attempted an actual definition of the word 'stress'. This is deliberate, because when people speak of stress, they tend to mean multiple things. We're aware that most people claim to experience stress. But when pressed, it is not always easy for them to ascertain what that stress is and what the symptoms are. Hence, in this chapter we have concentrated on the *experience* of stress. In the next one, we will attempt a definition.

 Getting personal

For **Susan**, life is to be lived, but she is slowly learning that this does not mean overstretching herself or heading towards burnout. Outside of work there are dinner parties to host, extended family members to visit, holidays to plan and work to do on the house. But she still has to be careful. Susan needs to learn that, despite what the advertisers promise, you cannot 'have it all'. It will take her a while to identify what relaxes her and plan to do it – writing it in the diary – and make space to ensure that she keeps life in biblical perspective.

Making a regular discipline of slowly praying through the priorities of the Lord's Prayer should help Susan to keep the Father's will, priorities and concerns uppermost in her mind.

I envy **Jack's** ability to relax, and in so many ways he seems to have understood the need to trust God and other people. He remains unfazed by the stresses experienced by many other people around him. As we've seen, he is not highly motivated by either money or career. It would be good if Jack could find energy and motivation to work in Christian ministry – the church needs individuals with his people skills! And he could do with remembering that praying for 'daily bread' might mean also playing his full role in domestic and other chores, so that Martha does not feel as though she has to carry the load by herself.

How would you try to advise Jack if you were his close friend?

4. The problem with the problem of stress

In 2010, a colleague and I cycled from Land's End to John O'Groats, a distance of nearly 1,000 miles. Naturally, we had a great sense of achievement when we finally arrived.

However, the exertion was intense. We were averaging nearly 90 miles per day, sometimes in extreme weather, and were always wondering whether it would be the bodies or the bikes that would give out first!

I recall trying to sleep on the third night of the ride. We had already cycled 250 miles. Generous hosts had provided us with a substantial meal and a pleasant evening of relaxation. But as I lay on the bed, my heart was pounding with such intensity that it felt like it was reverberating throughout my body. I could not sleep, but I really needed to in order to be ready for the next day. To me, it made no sense. I was exhausted, and yet my body would not relax.

Of course, the adrenaline that had enabled me to push up those steep hills and keep going despite wind and rain was still pumping through my body.

This happened every night. Eventually, I would relax, my heart rate would return to a normal rhythm, and I would be able to unwind. But that would only happen several days after completing the final push to the north-east of Scotland.

This, surely, is an example of stress that can motivate us and be good for us. But of course, such stress is only good if the body is allowed properly to recover once the pressure upon it is released. People have died while attempting this ride, and sometimes this has been because the body has been pressed beyond its ability.

I feel stressed when . . .

I have asked people to complete this simple sentence: 'I feel stressed when . . .' Most of these answers you know already:

- I feel unduly anxious about things.
- I feel out of control.
- I have more to do than the time available.
- I experience physical symptoms (for example, headache, stomach ache, neck ache).
- There is no space for recovery after a period of intense activity (either good or bad).

Defining stress is not straightforward, as we know. The list above includes stressful events and symptoms of stress, as well as the after-effects of stress. In the minds of most people, all stress is bad and very much part of life in the modern world. But I have deliberately waited until now to attempt a definition.

A 2010 Gallup Poll of American employees found that work-related stress was the most debilitating of all and that while job satisfaction had increased during the previous decade, so too had the volume of work and the sense that workers were not rewarded appropriately (financially or verbally).[1] Other surveys have pointed out that although twenty-first-century people have more labour-saving devices like dishwashers and increased access to pre-prepared food, their housework, cooking and domestic chores continue to occupy a considerable amount of our time. Yet, at the same time, electronic communication and a plethora of home recreation options are readily available, supposedly allowing us more entertainment and relaxation. Living in today's world feels very different from a generation ago.

We've looked at some of the factors that exacerbate modern stress: global travel, continual mobile phone and email connectivity, ever-widening circles of friends (many of whom are only connected through social media) and, importantly, inhabiting a world that never goes to sleep. All these contribute to the assumption that stress in the twenty-first century is considerably higher than it was even a few decades ago. Nevertheless, we concluded earlier that many of the psychological and physical symptoms of stress are not new.

Fight or flight?

The so-called 'fight-or-flight' phenomenon was a term that Dr Walter Cannon coined at the beginning of the twentieth century to describe an animal's reaction to actual or perceived threats.[2]

When confronted by danger, the body overcomes its tendency to freeze on the spot by releasing adrenaline and norepinephrine from the adrenal glands. This reaction, Cannon argued, was essential to motivate our ancestors to flee from wild animals or physical threats from the environment.

We continue to experience the fight-or-flight reaction when a surge of energy kicks in even though we may be extremely tired. Running for a bus, playing sport, racing to rescue a child from falling or submitting a bid just before a deadline all involve that rush of adrenaline.

The key point to note is that the adrenaline is rather like a fuel that needs to be burnt up. So when the fight-or-flight phenomenon is triggered by noise, bustle, busyness or anxiety rather than physical exertion, the adrenaline and resulting cortisol keep the body pumping, and do not allow it to return to a state of relaxation. It is rather like keeping the foot on the car's accelerator without engaging the clutch.

But, to continue that analogy, even when the clutch is engaged and the car is moving, the intensity must not be too severe or for too long, otherwise it may blow a gasket!

Martial arts instructor and life coach, Geoff Thompson, writes about this phenomenon in *Stress Buster: How to Stop Stress from Killing You*:

> Our ancestral instinct is badly outdated and gone crazy in a society exposed to more neurological stressors than ever before. The fight-or-flight instinct operates via the senses and triggers adrenaline (and other stress hormones such as cortisol) when it senses imminent danger. In theory this is fine; it prepares us for life and death battles with aggressors. In actuality it has major drawbacks because our senses are constantly being attacked by stimuli that might be aggressive but most often are not. Even the loud horn of a car can trigger fight or flight, releasing a cocktail of stress hormones in anticipation of an affray that never materializes.[3]

The difficulty of defining stress

We have already seen that one of the difficulties in trying to define stress is because we use the term fairly loosely. For example: 'I feel very stressed at the moment' (the amassing of several factors culminating in a feeling of being overwhelmed / out of control); 'I have a stress-headache' (caused by the tightening of neck muscles in reaction to challenging circumstances); 'moving house is one of the top five most stressful things that you will experience' (referring to a particularly exacting and demanding life event).[4]

The comments on stress above illustrate that the word is sometimes used to describe a list of stressful situations, and sometimes symptoms, where we feel out of control, overwhelmed or anxious, or experience physical afflictions. In reality, the two are related and one leads to the other: the stressful circumstances produce stressful effects upon us; the internal impact on the body is a result of the external pressure. This complicates the task of arriving at a definition. Our usage of the word 'depression' suffers from similar latitude, ranging from feelings / perception to a clinical definition, and in other contexts, the word can even refer to geography and finance.

Good stress, bad stress

In his book, *Adrenaline Stress*, Archibald Hart emphasizes the fact that certain types of people are more prone to stress than others. Stress is primarily (but by no means exclusively) the domain of the 'Type A' personality – the driven, ambitious individual.[5] Nevertheless, most people will also concede that a certain amount of pressure is required to complete tasks with a degree of energy and creativity. Our productivity increases when an essay deadline is approaching, or we need to be ready for an imminent presentation at work, or practise for the concert in which we are playing a lead part or warming up for that football game, or even getting our manuscript to an editor on time! We could call this 'good stress'. The dilemma, of course, is that the 'rush' that drives you to succeed at work, to compete in sports and to be generally productive in life is the very same drivenness and over-stretching that may cause another person to crack under the strain.

'Bad stress' is observable when we become irritable, un-productive or ill. If, instead of motivation and exhilaration, the stress-event produces debilitation and exerts a negative effect, then most people would agree that this is bad stress. It has become popular to concentrate on the negative effect of adrenaline and cortisol and their impact on the body. The reality, however, is that one person's stress might just be the 'sweet spot' of another person's creativity, but having the discernment to know the difference is not straightforward. Moreover, the 'Type A' personality will seek out ever more stimulation, and even addictive stress-fixes, because they enjoy the adrenaline rush.

Is there a neat distinction between good stress and bad stress? And surely too much of a good thing also has negative consequences? Similar to the analogy of stretching a rubber band earlier is that of a bow and arrow. The bow needs to be pulled tight, putting stress on the cord in order for there to be enough tension to propel the arrow through the air. So long as the cord is not pulled too tightly, it will return to its usual elasticity and serve its purpose again. Overstretching the cord might result in it snapping or losing its shape. The analogies of snapping and losing shape (weight gain/loss?) could apply equally to stress in the human being.

We all understand that if you overstretch for too long, you will snap. Remember, though, that I have mentioned that the cord will also lose elasticity if it is pulled taut (but not necessarily overstretched) for too long a period without being allowed to go slack. The human body can bounce back from intense stress if the tension is relieved and the body is allowed to return to its less stressful state.

I noticed a concerning trend among the young professionals in my former parish in south London. 'Work hard/play hard' was the mantra for many. However, I also detected that many of them didn't last long working in the city – perhaps ten to fifteen years. By their late thirties, having lived life at full stretch, they lost their bounce, and stress started to take its toll.

Experts have pointed out that a moderate amount of stress produces other drugs in the body, such as insulin and serotonin, which we need. Elisabeth Wilson observes that

> a bit of stress isn't necessarily terrible . . . stress forces you to make decisions, take responsibility . . . [it] protects us from falling into a state of depression. A recent study found that small doses of the stress hormone cortisol protects some people against depression in the way that anti-depressants regulate mood. Too much cortisol leads to extreme exhaustion . . . the body's hormones work in delicate balance. When the three main stress hormones (adrenaline, noradrenalin and cortisol) are fired they affect the levels of others.[6]

Cortisol gets you out of bed in the morning. But chronically elevated cortisol causes depression. So, stress is not all bad. Rather, it needs to be managed and made to work for, not against, you.

Pinning down the definition

Put simply, stress is the body's reaction to anything requiring a physical, mental or emotional change or response. Stress is the body's response to environmental demands or pressures.[7]

But this is a rather all-encompassing summary. Without being more specific, I am not sure how such a definition might help me deal with my daily feelings of stress.

The Health and Safety Executive's formal definition of work-related stress is as follows:

> The adverse reaction people have to excessive pressures or other types of demand placed on them at work. Stress is not an illness – it is a state. However, if stress becomes too excessive and prolonged, mental and physical illness may develop.[8]

To return to the simplest of stress definitions: a person experiences stress when they perceive that the demands of their work are greater than their ability to cope. Yes, this is certainly true of the working world that many of us inhabit. However, what about the stress that comes from family tension, from the daily commute and from noise pollution? Much of my stress is often not directly the fault of anyone around me, but just part of the world in which I live.

Archibald Hart argues that dealing with stress is primarily to do with unlearning an addiction to adrenaline and ensuring that you are not always looking for that 'high'. However, it should be noted that adrenaline (epinephrine) is blamed for 'depression, mania, stress, OCD, psychopathy . . . and it is not only the "Type A" who are suffering from the need for an adrenaline "rush"'.[9]

We feel stressed when we feel that 'things are out of control'.[10] This definition is simple, but it is also fairly comprehensive: when an individual feels overstretched and under-resourced, then they are stressed.

Making stress work for you

Back in 1908, psychologists Robert Yerkes and John Dodson observed the performance of individuals when stimulated either physically or mentally.

They noticed a definite increase in performance after 'arousal', but found that after the stimulus, it peters out. This subsequently became known as the Yerkes/Dodson arousal-performance curve. Their research found that different tasks required different levels of arousal for optimal performance. For example, difficult or intellectually demanding tasks may require a lower level of arousal (to facilitate concentration), whereas tasks demanding stamina or persistence may be better performed with higher levels of arousal (to increase motivation). This is graphically demonstrated as a bell curve, which varies a little according to the subject's familiarity with the task (the harder/less familiar it is, the steeper the 'spike').

But in each instance, the climb up the bell curve is stimulating and energizing. The downward climb is draining and negative, affecting performance, interest and attention. This research gives a helpful insight into why we feel energized by certain events/tasks and why we might feel 'flat' even after positive stresses – for example, after we get back from a good holiday, or the Monday blues after an exciting weekend.[11]

'Christian' stresses

We can add what I consider to be particular Christian stresses to this list:

- **The task that God has given us is impossible.** We are
  called to go into all the world and make disciples of all
  nations (see Matthew 28:18–20). But that task is never
  completed; the world is not yet won! Unfinished tasks
  create stress.
- **Evangelical ministry is task oriented.** There is a world
  to win for Christ, involving speaking and service. How
  do I know when I've achieved anything? And how do I
  live with the task that is yet undone?
- **God calls for perfection.** Jesus' instruction to 'be
  perfect as your heavenly father is perfect' is in fact an
  echo of: 'be holy for I am holy' (Matthew 5:48). Striving
  to be perfect can make one feel driven and dissatisfied.
- **The Christian leader is to be above reproach**
  (1 Timothy 3:2). Does this not disqualify everyone
  from ministry?
- **Leaders like to be in control.** Most stress is the feeling
  of being out of control.

Many of these perceived stresses are based on a misunderstanding of the provision God has made for our failures. Our
confidence should rest not on our ability to do God's work,
but rather on God's character and his own commitment to
work all things for his glory.

Remember that God is:

- **omnipotent**: God is all-powerful; we are not
- **omniscient**: God knows the end from the beginning
  even when we struggle to make sense of life (he also
  provides for failure)
- **omnipresent**: as he gives his disciples the enormous
  task of making disciples of all nations, he also promises,
  'I am with you always' (Matthew 28:20).

I cannot be 'omni-competent'; rather, I should be utterly dependent on the resources that God provides me with to live the Christian life for the long haul. Understanding God's character helps me to live with the incomplete task of evangelizing the world and the impossible demand of being perfect.

Striving for a good work/life balance

One of my students once asked me, 'Can you teach me to relax?' It was an interesting question, to say the least, given that I felt I had been going through one of the most demanding periods of my life. I was tempted to say, 'Look at the swan and remember what is going on below the surface as it glides across the lake!' However, this highly intelligent and productive student had noted that I had posted on my Facebook page the various family activities that we had enjoyed in recent weeks, and genuinely wanted to know how to maintain a healthy work/life balance. I am not convinced that I have great wisdom here: in fact, most of us write books on such topics largely because we are striving to arrive at the answer and are hoping we will get there by the conclusion of the book! The one comment I did make, however, which seemed to help, was: 'I have learned not to feel guilty when I do not work, and I know that I need to relax in order to be more productive.'

Arriving at this remark had taken time (remember chapter 1). But I now realize that the problem of stress still remains largely *internal* rather than *external*. I firmly believe that our minds, hearts, attitudes and emotions need to be recalibrated with good biblical theology about God, love, worship, Christian service and security in God's good purposes for us and for the world. In a sense, when we get those things sorted out, stress looks after itself.

When we feel stressed, we often tend to go for false fixes.

Using caffeine, sugar or alcohol to get us through the day or help us unwind is part of society's instinctive reaction to pressure and tiredness. However, these are short-term remedies at best. In fact, sugar might give us a quick burst of energy, but the effects quickly dissipate (it is better to eat complex carbohydrates, which slowly release energy), and drinking alcohol to relax can lead to a dangerous dependency and, also, depress rather than stimulate us.

In this book, I am determined to concentrate on healthier ways to alleviate stress, ways that will result from changes to our thinking and attitudes (to ourselves and our circumstances), and changes in our behaviour and our health (looking after our well-being and spiritual needs).

Paul talked about 'learning the secret of contentment':

> I know what it is to be in need, and I know what it is to have plenty. I have learned the secret of being content in any and every situation, whether well fed or hungry, whether living in plenty or in want. I can do all this through him who gives me strength.
> (Philippians 4:12–13)

Sounds easy, right? We will delve into some of these themes in the following chapters.

 Getting personal

For me, this now gets personal. It is easy to bring to mind some stressful days in the last couple of years. Only with the benefit of hindsight can I see some of the factors that contributed to that feeling of being stressed. And also, with the clarity of hindsight, I can think about some things that I would now do differently. How about you? There may be things that you too would do differently upon later reflection.

Certainly, taking the time regularly to concentrate on God's good character and asking him to change me into the kind of person he wants me to be is a good place to start. And starting here should mean that when the next stressful day comes, I will have more resources to handle the pressure better.

Some of this chapter is written with **Thomas** in mind. Has he learned the secret of contentment? He needs to find a way of living that is not dependent on the adrenaline or sugar rush. He could perhaps set his sights lower in some areas of life and be grateful for what he has and all he has already achieved. This will not happen overnight, but it will be essential if he wants to keep going for the long haul.

It is quite understandable that **Anna** feels the stress of modern living. Her whole life is spent trying to be in control. I think she may take some persuading, but, given the chance, I would encourage her to find some time for herself. For some mothers of young children, time in the bathroom is the only chance to be alone. Maybe Anna could keep a helpful Christian book by the bath and have a long soak while reading some devotional thoughts. I am convinced that she will be better able to give quality time to her young twins and her husband if she first brings her burdens to God.

Both Thomas and Anna benefit from good stress. They might well think about finding an accountability partner to help them identify (and deal with) the bad stuff.

5. Worry and refocusing

Bobby McFerrin wrote and sang iconic words in 1988: 'Don't worry, be happy.' The song encapsulates the innate desire for relief from stress: the laid-back rhythm, the gentle distraction and the swaying melody, assisted by an escapism of your choice. Perhaps a sun-kissed beach, good music and relaxed and uncluttered time: all essential ingredients for true happiness, right?

Corrie ten Boom was a Dutch Christian who sheltered many Jews from the Nazi Holocaust during the Second World War, but was eventually caught and imprisoned. Her book, *The Hiding Place*, tells her nail-biting story. Reflecting on the challenges of living the Christian life under extreme pressure, she wrote some wonderful words of encouragement:

> Worrying is carrying tomorrow's load with today's strength – carrying two days at once. It is moving into tomorrow ahead of time. Worrying doesn't empty tomorrow of its sorrow. It empties today of its strength.[1]

Long before I had studied any Greek or Latin, I assumed that the 'beatitudes' at the beginning of the Sermon on the Mount (Matthew 5:3–12) were so named because they encapsulated a combination of 'being' (security in our relationship with God) and 'attitude' (our outlook on life). Of course, the English word comes in fact from the Latin word *beātitūdō*, which means 'blessedness'.[2]

Nevertheless, it is worth noticing that freedom from worry, and happiness according to Jesus' teaching, are attained by reorienting our lives so that they line up with God's good plans and purposes for us. Indeed, this is a combination of being a different person and having a new attitude to life, so in that respect, it is a 'be-attitude'!

Worry – a huge problem

Worry has been defined as a negative effect, associated with a perceived inability to control or obtain desired results in forthcoming situations.[3] Anxiety is the word that best describes much of what, in colloquial English, we call 'worry'. However, anxiety can cover a range of physiological ailments; panic and phobia are the words most used for short-lived concerns, whereas worry tends to be used to describe an ongoing perceived state of anxiety / uncertainty. When worry is severe, doctors call this 'generalized anxiety disorder', because it does not have a fixed or limited focus.

Worry and anxiety can result in long-term health effects, and for some people generalized anxiety disorder can be debilitating, not to mention a huge medical drain due to the costs of treating it.[4] As well as robbing us of our tranquillity and general peace of mind, ongoing anxiety can be responsible for an increase in heart disease.[5] Even at a less drastic level, the everyday experience of worry results in sleeplessness, irritability, loss of appetite / overeating, and other physical and psychosomatic complaints.

Faced with the perception that life is out of control, life's worries circulate around the mind, draining away our productivity and leaving us to daydream of that elusive romantic tropical escape.

However, the answer that Jesus gives to worry is not escapism. His answer in the Sermon on the Mount deals very much with the reality of living in a stressful world.

'Therefore I tell you, do not worry about your life, what you will eat or drink; or about your body, what you will wear. Is not life more than food, and the body more than clothes? Look at the birds of the air; they do not sow or reap or store away in barns, and yet your heavenly Father feeds them. Are you not much more valuable than they? Can any one of you by worrying add a single hour to your life?

'And why do you worry about clothes? See how the flowers of the field grow. They do not labour or spin. Yet I tell you that not even Solomon in all his splendour was dressed like one of these. If that is how God clothes the grass of the field, which is here today and tomorrow is thrown into the fire, will he not much more clothe you – you of little faith? So do not worry, saying, "What shall we eat?" or "What shall we drink?" or "What shall we wear?" For the pagans run after all these things, and your heavenly Father knows that you need them. But seek first his kingdom and his righteousness, and all these things will be given to you as well. Therefore do not worry about tomorrow, for tomorrow will worry about itself. Each day has enough trouble of its own.'

(Matthew 6:25–34)

Three stress-relieving attitudes

1. Remember who is boss
Jesus says, 'No-one can serve two masters' (Matthew 6:24). The principle he enunciates seems to apply beyond the specific issue of money. The Greek word, translated as 'Mammon' in older Bible versions, refers to the way in which the acquisition of wealth takes on a religious form. This is evident in much modern living: the pursuit of wealth absorbs my best energies; the acquisition of 'things' becomes an end in and of itself; I work for holidays, housing and pampering myself. Mammon becomes a substitute god.

The command 'do not worry' brings little comfort to the worrier. In fact, it can add another worry to the already long list of worries! Unless, of course, there is a good reason given for not worrying, which Jesus quite clearly offers in this passage. 'Resolve in your own mind,' he seems to be saying, 'who is the master of your fate.' What comfort there is in those four words: 'your heavenly Father knows . . .' (v. 32). 'Such knowledge is too wonderful for me' (Psalm 139:6). Moreover, if we resolve in our mind to seek first God's kingdom and his righteousness, as a daily and moment-by-moment reflex action, he promises that everything else will slot into place (v. 33). Once God is retained as the rightful Lord of our lives, everything else is put in its proper perspective. This is the number-one priority.

2. File away each day's cares and watch your thoughts
The principle that Jesus enunciates is: 'Each day has enough trouble of its own' (Matthew 6:34).

As we shall see in a moment, part of dealing with this kind of stress has to do with turning off our racing mind. Remember: no matter how hard you press the car's accelerator, if it is not in gear and the clutch is not engaged, nothing will happen (apart from you burning a lot of unnecessary fuel). Worry is a bit like that.

We find it hard to stop our hearts racing. I think of the late nights I spent fishing under the pier heads in Jersey. Constantly anticipating that the float would go under with a big bite was mesmerizing. Well into the night, the time came to pack up and go home to bed. But my overactive mind would be full of the glow of the pier head lights, as I imagined fish swimming round and round. Fishing (at least of this sort) is one of the least stressful things a person can do, and in reality I still find it a great stress reliever. Nevertheless, in order to get a good night's sleep, something needed to be turned off in my mind after my late-night fishing. How much more so when there are worries about issues of greater importance. Worry and stress operate on a self-perpetuating cycle.

The answer to this kind of stress involves somehow breaking the thought cycle. As has often been wryly observed: 'Worrying is like a rocking chair, it gives you something to do, but it gets you nowhere.' And: 'Who said worry never achieved anything? None of the things I ever worried about actually happened!'

I recently read a magazine article about a survey on worry, which revealed that 40% of the things most people worry about never happen; 30% of what we worry about has already happened and cannot be changed; 22% of what we worry about regards problems beyond our control; and only 8% of what we worry about involves situations over which we have any influence.[6] I am sure that the results are likely to be correct.

It is fascinating that Jesus highlights food and fashion (food, drink and clothing, Matthew 6:28–31) as the things that pagans actively pursue. If we were to remove the television programmes and magazine articles dedicated to food and fashion from our media, there would be a lot less to watch and read! Remember that God knows your needs, and has assured us that he likes to hear our prayer for 'daily bread' (Matthew 6:11). Remember too that the far-distant future is largely out of your control. Today has enough trouble of its own.

Learning not to worry begins with a choice to break the worry-cycle and instead to trust God. Biblical passages reinforce this priority.

We are advised in Psalm 37:

> Do not fret because of those who are evil
>   or be envious of those who do wrong . . .
> Trust in the LORD and do good . . .
> Take delight in the LORD,
>   and he will give you the desires of your heart.
> Commit your way to the LORD;
>   trust in him and he will do this:
> he will make your righteous reward shine like the dawn.
> (Psalm 37:1–6)

In other words, as Jesus says, seek God first and then all other things will slot into place.

God promises to meet our needs, not our wants. We read in Philippians 4:19: 'And my God will meet all your needs according to the riches of his glory in Christ Jesus.' God will give us our daily bread, not our daily caviar.

When Martha tried to get Jesus involved in a domestic tussle over sharing household chores with her sister, Jesus rebuked her. '"Martha, Martha," the Lord answered, "you are worried and upset about many things, but only one thing is needed. Mary has chosen what is better, and it will not be taken away from her"' (Luke 10:41–42). Don't worry about the household to the extent that you fail to live for God today; the house may well need cleaning again tomorrow, and food will need cooking again. It's better not to lose sleep over it. Choose wisely and sit at Jesus' feet while you have the time.

3. Distinguish between what you can and cannot control

I might die when I am fifty-five; I might die when I am seventy-five. (It is now too late to worry about dying in my forties!) We cannot control the whole of our life. In my experience, it is those who think that they can control everything who end up the most stressed. Worry will not add a single hour to your life – in fact, it is more likely to have the opposite effect!

Of course, there are lots of things that I *can* control; the way I react to stress, Jesus seems to be saying, is one of them. Have you noticed that two people faced with the same circumstances might respond very differently? My conviction in writing this book (as we've already seen) is that the change needs to begin on the inside, at the level of my thinking and attitude to God and his world. And remembering that God is the Master of my fate, not me, is obviously an important part of this process.

Practical advice and biblical wisdom

1. Turn your anxieties into prayer

> Cast all your anxiety on him because he cares for you.
> (1 Peter 5:7)

Popular books on stress extol the benefit of meditation.[7] Even a modest twenty minutes per day, concentrating on the discipline of emptying the mind of distracting thoughts and allowing relaxation to work its way through the body, is proven to be beneficial both emotionally and physically.[8] At one level, there is wisdom here, although the Christian emphasis on meditation tends to concentrate not on emptying the mind, but rather on filling it with wholesome thoughts. For example:

> Finally, brothers and sisters, whatever is true, whatever
> is noble, whatever is right, whatever is pure, whatever is
> lovely, whatever is admirable – if anything is excellent or
> praiseworthy – think about such things . . . And the God
> of peace will be with you.
> (Philippians 4:8, 9)

Alongside meditation is prayer. Meditation stills your heart, while 'Prayer turns over the responsibility to God – and leaves it there. Every evening I turn my worries over to God. He's going to be up all night anyway' (Mary C. Crowley).[9]

For the Christian, prayer is more than a stress-buster. It is built on the confidence that God delights to hear the cries of his children and that he intervenes in our circumstances when we pray.

A few practical points have helped me. Firstly, be specific in prayer. It is often the silly little details of life that clutter up my mind. And I tend to think that God is too busy running the world for me to involve him in them. But I do believe that Jesus' reference to God's detailed knowledge and care of sparrows and flowers (Matthew 6:26, 28) should encourage me to bring the smallest details of life to him too. The second thing that I have found helpful is to 'pray continually' (1 Thessalonians 5:17). Of course, this does not mean that we should spend our whole time verbalizing before God our needs and wants (although more of this would be good). It does not have to be on our knees, eyes closed and hands together either – moreover, closing your eyes while driving is never a good idea, albeit the place where I (and sometimes my passengers) do some of our praying! Rather, I think Paul's instruction to the Thessalonian Christians is similar to that expressed in Revelation 3:20 where Jesus says, 'Here I am! I stand at the door and knock. If anyone hears my voice and opens the door, I will come in and eat with them, and they with me.' To a church that has shut Jesus out of its life and become lukewarm, Jesus says, 'Let me in!' O. Hallesby's classic book on prayer emphasizes that Jesus wants to be involved in all of our life; we open the door so we may commune with him constantly.[10]

2. Rebuild your confidence in God's character

Related to the first point is our need to break the worry cycle by constantly focusing on our Father. Jesus alludes to God's care. If he cares even for the sparrow, how much more does he cares for you? You are loved and invited into God's presence, hence Matthew 7:9–11:

> 'Which of you, if your son asks for bread, will give him a stone? Or if he asks for a fish, will give him a snake? If you, then, though you are evil, know how to give good gifts to your children, how much more will your Father in heaven give good gifts to those who ask him!'

Jesus also speaks of the Father's providence: 'He knows you need these things' (v. 32b) and 'all these things will be given to you as well' (v. 33b). Before you can pray with confidence, you need to remember that God is King, and that he continues his sovereignly rule over his world. We should repent of our failure to acknowledge this fact. Then we will find that knowing God to be in absolute control will give us great confidence in prayer. So, we humble ourselves before God and acknowledge that his hand is mighty, and our anxiety dissipates when we realize that he truly cares (1 Peter 5:6–7) (more on this in chapters 10, 11 and 12).

3. Live for today and plan for tomorrow

I have found the principle of living for today and planning for tomorrow to be very liberating.

Planning, of course, does not militate against trusting God for daily bread. There is a plethora of examples of Jesus and Paul planning their ministries, albeit with a high degree of flexibility as the Father brought about circumstantial changes. So, I am not at all proposing reckless living with no concern for the future. But rather, we should take seriously the fact that God has promised to provide for each day as it happens.

You might like to think of the 'manna principle' (Exodus 16). The Israelites were instructed only to collect enough manna for each day's need (with double the amount on the day before the Sabbath). It was an act of faith that God would provide enough for one day at a time.

Personally, when planning, I live by lists. I used to find that my mind was very ill-disciplined (it actually still is, rather). I would start to pray but would then think, 'Did I put the dustbin out? Did I write that email to a colleague? Oh, I need to pay that cheque into the bank . . .' It was as if my mind had been seeking to get my attention all day, and finally I had slowed down to pray and it jumped in! However, once I pause and write down the distractions, I am then able to concentrate on prayer. Living in a modern world with a vast number of unfinished tasks, we need to find a way of filtering them out of our conscious memory in order to revisit them later.[11]

All three of the above points are interlinked.

We have already seen how Jesus found space alone to pray very early in the morning (Mark 1:35–37), and he prioritized preaching the gospel over healing. Similarly, after a night of prayer, Jesus was ready for his accusers (and his sleeping disciples were not) when they came to arrest him in Mark 14.

God grant me grace . . .

The 'Serenity Prayer' has been used by Alcoholics Anonymous to encapsulate their desire to help an alcoholic towards personal recovery and continued sobriety through group fellowship and support. It is designed to encourage the person praying to get back in control of their life. The form in which it is prayed is as follows:

> God grant me the serenity
> To accept the things I cannot change,
> Courage to change the things I can.
> And the wisdom to know the difference.

Reinhold Niebuhr claims to have authored the prayer, but also acknowledges that there may have been versions of it in existence before this. The fuller version of the prayer clearly shows that the Christian guide to serenity is not found in self-help, or even in group help, but rather in a wholehearted confidence that God has borne our burdens and thus can assure us of happiness.

> God, give us grace to accept with serenity
> the things that cannot be changed,
> Courage to change the things
> which should be changed,
> and the wisdom to distinguish
> the one from the other.
> Living one day at a time,

Enjoying one moment at a time,

Accepting hardship as a pathway to peace,

Taking, as Jesus did,

This sinful world as it is,

Not as I would have it,

Trusting that You will make all things right,

If I surrender to Your will,

So that I may be reasonably happy in this life,

And supremely happy with You forever in the next.

Amen.[12]

For anyone suffering from worry or anxiety, these are surely good words to pray.

The following very practical tips on prayer and planning help alleviate worry, and therefore also stress.

Practical tips

1. **Pray daily.** As a young Christian, I was strongly encouraged to have a 'quiet time'. This is a daily slot (perhaps best in the morning) for reading a portion of Scripture and praying through its implications, bringing the demands of the day ahead before the Lord. It is a practice that I have continued throughout my life, and I know that when I short-change this discipline, my day seems full of anxieties and stress. May I encourage you to revive the practice if you have let it slip? Use it as an opportunity to leave your burdens at the foot of the cross and instead take up God's priorities.

2. **Plan thoroughly.** Resolve each day to plan and prioritize. A short time spent thinking through upcoming tasks, noting down everything that needs doing and shunning interruptions that distract will bring huge relief. There is always something quite satisfying about ticking off a 'to-do' or 'next-action' list!

3. **Ponder persistently.** Time spent considering the promise of the Father's care should increase our confidence that '. . . my God will meet all your needs according to the riches of his glory in Christ Jesus' (Philippians 4:19). Remember God's faithfulness and thank him for answers to prayer.

 Getting personal

Susan has made some wise decisions. After her period off work due to anxiety, she is better placed to arrange her life and now has a better sense of proportion. Having made considerable amounts of money in the past, she will need to reduce her expectations of expensive holidays and fine dining. However, deep down she knows that this is all worth it, as her new career gives her much more enjoyment. Her pension will not be as large as it might have been, but it will be adequate. When she finds herself worrying about the future, she should try to train herself to take pleasure in the good changes she has made, which now enhance her life.

Anna feels she spends too much time worrying. This manifests itself in the questions that swim around her mind, such as: 'Will we earn enough to pay the mortgage?' and 'Will the children be healthy, happy and stable?' These keep her awake at night and mean that often she cannot relax and enjoy the moment during the day. Quite obviously, there can be real threats to our happiness. But I hope that Anna will find some time each day to unburden herself to God and leave her worries on his broad shoulders.

How would you advise Anna, in the light of this chapter?

6. Don't let the sun go down on your anger

I like the story about the man who wanted to borrow his neighbour's lawnmower. As he made his way to his neighbour's front door, he rehearsed what he would say: 'I'm not sure I know him well enough to ask him for a loan . . . He might not be that keen on the idea of lending me his mower anyway . . . He's a crotchety character too, so he will probably say "no" . . .' The man worked himself into such a frenzy that, by the time he arrived at his neighbour's front door, he was agitated and convinced he would receive a negative reception. The door opened, and he found himself blurting out to his perplexed neighbour, 'I didn't want to borrow your lawnmower anyway . . .', before storming back home!

If, at its most basic root, stress has to do with our need for control, then anger, like worry, often manifests itself when we feel out of control. This means that our mental attitude towards stress, as we have seen, is all-important. But other factors also affect us.

I feel most stressed when I have had too little sleep, or I am hungry, or I am overworked and under-recognized, or I feel hurt or directionless. This will often spill over into angry outbursts. But generally, I am the last person to recognize that fact. As far as I am concerned, it is all the other people in the world who have a problem. Also, it is strange how some days everyone around me seems to be angrier. Just look at all those terrible, aggressive drivers on the road; I'd like to give them a piece of my mind!

A friend of mine, the evangelist Vijay Menon, likes to say that when his church council came to meet together, everyone had 'bees in their bonnet'; they were all a-buzz with issues and problems that they wanted to bring to the council. They consequently started convening for half an hour of prayer before each meeting and found that by the time they got to the business agenda, all the bees were dead.[1]

I do believe that God changes the world through prayer. Hence, the consistent priority – by teaching and example – of prayer. Nevertheless, the prime impact of prayer is that, through prayer, God changes *me*. You too may have noticed how different the world looks when you seek first God's kingdom and his righteousness (see Matthew 6:33). I rise from my knees, and the irritating and unreasonable people have disappeared, and I see my fellow human beings in a new light.

A stressful world is full of angry people

It often seems that people are angrier than they used to be. Management consultants run anger management workshops on how to defuse office tension. The Speaker in the House of Commons has to rein in intemperate outbursts. Peaceful protests on the street turn violent as people vent their frustration.

I suspect that one of the reasons why the world feels angrier is because our modern way of life enables us to communicate instantly and globally, with no necessary thought or regard for the human relationships that might be involved.[2]

If you remove the relationship with someone, then you are able to bypass any awareness of how they may respond to what you are saying, so you can vent your anger and frustration. Once in relationship with someone, language is likely to become more tempered and measured.

For example, read any news article online and then look at the thread of reader comments afterwards. Some of the vitriol and venom is shocking. And yet, meet those same people face to face, and most would never dream of speaking in such a cavalier or aggressive way. As one writer has put it, 'A perfect storm engenders online rudeness, including virtual anonymity and thus a lack of accountability, physical distance and the medium of writing.'[3]

In 2013, there was a media controversy related to Twitter posts directed at the feminist campaigner, Caroline Criado-Perez, and Member of Parliament, Stella Creasy, because they lobbied for a famous female face to be printed on the new banknotes. Torrents of abuse, including threats of rape and murder, came their way. The finger of blame has been pointed at the need for censorship by the social media organization itself, and Twitter have attempted to absolve themselves by saying that it is the individuals involved who should be punished.[4] Fair point. However, providing a medium for uncensored and anonymous hate speech should also, perhaps, be considered culpable. Twitter eventually conceded this point by suspending the accounts of abusers and clarifying the company's commitment to internet safety.[5]

Of course, this is not the same thing as saying that anger is caused by the relative anonymity of what we are able to say on Facebook or Twitter. However, it does illustrate the point that there is a two-way link between a broken relationship contributing to anger, and anger being allowed to be expressed and left unchecked where there is no relationship with the person against whom you are venting it. Anger can be directed inwardly at myself: I am frustrated when I am unable to do what I want to do or to organize and live my life in the way that I want. More likely, however, my anger is directed at someone else, either the person whom I perceive to be directly thwarting my plans or someone else who gets in the way between me and them! Many people are angry at God, rather like Jonah was (in Jonah 4), because they perceive God to be acting in a way that they do not think is appropriate for him to behave.

Need I say more? Anger is a huge problem. Moreover, anger gives fuel to stress by pumping adrenaline and cortisol around the body, robbing us of tranquillity, sleep and a sense of control, and it can leave a trail of wounded people in our wake. At its most extreme, human anger is responsible for aggression, violence and even murder.

In your anger, do not sin

Ephesians 4:26 contains some very practical advice: 'In your anger do not sin: do not let the sun go down while you are still angry.' If you go to bed angry, you won't sleep. First, sort it out; then with a clear conscience you will be more likely to sleep.

But the verse is saying much more. Paul quotes from Psalm 4. The verse is set in the context of dealing fairly and faithfully with our neighbour, practically displacing anger (and other sins, v. 31) with conversation that will build people up and not tear them down (v. 29), and acting in kindness, compassion and forgiveness (vv. 28, 32). Significantly, my anger is brought into check when God is first in control of my heart.

As we will see in a moment, there are times when God is righteously angry, because we mortal beings attempt to dethrone him and puff ourselves up. God has the supreme right to govern all of his creatures, and any attempt to put ourselves on the throne will be strongly resisted. Despite our wilful rebellion, God is compassionate and merciful, and slow to anger.[6] God's wrath is turned away when our sin is forgiven. This happens when, by faith, we personally apprehend the benefits of Jesus' atoning death for us (see Romans 3:21–26 for more on this).

God's wrath is turned away and our sin is forgiven, so it logically follows that our love for God flows over into love, forgiveness and compassion towards our neighbour. Simplistic? Maybe. But some of the best stress defusion is not complex, but rather requires active day-by-day steps. Start by thinking about the relationships that should be healed and built up with words and actions, and try not to speak into an anonymous vacuum. Meditate on the goodness and grace of God, praying that your character would be shaped by who God is. It is always wise to pause before writing an angry email or making a hasty phone call, in order to ensure that what you are about to say is not clouded by personal hurt.

When upsets and frustrations are buried, rather than being addressed and dealt with, they become like swallowed dynamite. They will eventually spark off a huge explosion!

'Misunderstanding and mishandling'

In the context of anger, John T. Hower observed,

> man has a natural response of indignation at unrighteousness, but his distorted view of unrighteousness often results in an anger response due to unfounded reasons.[7]

Ephesians 4:26–27 seems to concede that anger is n[
wrong (*in* your anger do not sin). And in order to cor[
appropriate outlet for stress and anger today, we need to begin
with the fact that God consistently expresses anger.

God's anger

The second commandment speaks of God as a jealous God
who punishes sin (see Exodus 20:5). But he does not fly off
the handle or lash out in rage and subsequently regret it. Nor
is he threatened by another person's success or prominence.
His jealousy arises out of indignation that any other creature
should presume to attempt to usurp his rightful place as the
Creator. He is God by right, the One who absolutely deserves
our worship. And to dethrone God is not to stamp on his
foolish pride but rather to fail to give him the honour and
worth that are his due. But theologian J. I. Packer helpfully
makes the point that we should think of God's jealousy as red,
not green.[8] God is hot with indignation, not green with envy.

Jesus' anger at the abuse of the temple was driven by zeal
(John 2:17; the word 'zeal' is from the same root word for
'jealousy'), because its true purpose as a house of prayer
(Matthew 21:13) was being abused. Jesus was angry towards
Pharisaic Sabbath observance, which failed to recognize the
work of God (Mark 3:5).

God's wrath is revealed against godlessness, wickedness and
suppressing the truth (Romans 1:18). So, personal anger is part
of God's character. Thus, when human beings long for justice
and are indignant at injustice, in some respects, they are
reflecting the character of God.

We have already noted that God is slow to anger. He rebukes
Jonah for his anger at the wicked city of Nineveh, showing
that he (God) is far more compassionate than his reluctant

prophet. God is angry at injustice, and his anger is displayed when his honour is defamed.

Thus, we should infer, there is a real place for human anger, particularly when it is concerned about God's honour and at the obvious and appalling injustices in the world. The Christian psychologist, Charles E. Cerling Jr, is therefore right, I believe, when he says, 'If we attempt to justify the anger of God, then there must be some justification for human anger.'[9]

Similarly, John E. Pedersen asks,

> Is love itself a sin? Is compassion? I think we must answer 'no'. The emotions involved are not wrong in themselves; it is the way in which they are expressed that the opportunity lies . . .[10]

Human anger – warnings against

I am very adept at justifying my own anger. Much harder, however, is the attempt to evaluate whether it's personal pique or self-righteous indignation that are the sparks that ignite my anger. As a wise person observed:

> Anybody can become angry – that is easy; but to be angry with the right person, and to the right degree, and at the right time, and for the right purpose, and in the right way – that is not within everybody's power and is not easy.[11]

The Bible also has a lot of warnings about the abuse of anger.

Although Ephesians 4:26 (quoting Psalm 4:4) seems to justify anger, it then immediately qualifies it.[12] Cerling makes the point that this verse should be read in the context of the sins that are obviously condemned without qualification in this paragraph: putting off falsehood, not stealing, not being idle.[13] John Calvin further elucidates:

There are three faults by which we offend God in being angry. This is when we are angry from the slight causes, and often from none, or are moved by private injuries or offenses. The second is when we go too far, and are carried into intemperate excesses. The third is when our anger which ought to have been turned against ourselves or against sins, is turned against our brethren.[14]

Thomas Aquinas spoke of anger as a strong passion: 'A passion of the sensitive appetite is good insofar as it is regulated by reason, whereas it is evil if it sets the order of reason aside.'[15]

Temper your anger

Desmond Tutu wisely remarked, 'My father always used to say, "Don't raise your voice. Improve your argument." Good sense does not always lie with the loudest shouters, nor can we say that a large, unruly crowd is always the best arbiter of what is right.'[16]

God has every right to be angry: the world he made has spurned its Maker. But he is consistently described as being 'slow to anger and abounding in love' (Numbers 14:18; Psalms 103:8; 145:8). The Christian too should be slow to anger. We should listen first and be slower to speak (James 1:19; cf. Ecclesiastes 7:9; Proverbs 16:32). This is particularly true for those in Christian leadership (Titus 1:9). As I said at the beginning of this chapter, it is very hard for me to see the whole world objectively; my reactions (including angry ones) are swayed by many things other than a sense of protectiveness about God's honour. So, don't be quick to lash out, even if it's only with your tongue, because, in this regard, God is slow, and we should mimic him.

Though there are exceptions, the weight of the biblical teaching on anger is negative (Matthew 5:22; Romans 12:19; 2 Corinthians 12:20; Galatians 5:20; Ephesians 4:31; Colossians 3:8; James 1:20). This would imply that the New Testament writers are cautious about an immediate assumption that our anger is justifiable. Before we feel the right to express our indignation, we need first to examine our hearts. Clearly, then, anger needs to be brought under control.[17]

But as with other aspects of stress, I do not believe that the Christian answer is merely a Herculean effort or pulling oneself up by the bootlaces. Here are three practical Christian principles for dealing with anger.

Practical principles

1. Ask God to control your heart

Stressed Christians are often disciplined people. They have committed themselves to changing their mind and outlook by aligning their thinking with God's plans and priorities. They have determined that their actions should be reflective of the character of God and they diligently seek to follow his commands. They can control their thinking; they can control their actions. But none of us can easily control our reactions. There is simply not enough time when you drop a brick on your toe to control the words that flow out of your mouth!

Our reactions to difficult circumstances may reveal – perhaps to our own surprise – the true state of our hearts. Jesus said '. . . the mouth speaks what the heart is full of' (Luke 6:45). If I want my reactions to be better aligned with God's ways and purposes, I need to ask God to guard and control my heart. Thus, anger should primarily be vented vertically (God-ward) rather than horizontally (at other humans); we will need to train ourselves to learn this reflex reaction. This does not, of course, mean that we should spend our time ranting at God, but it does mean that when we do turn our anger heavenwards, we are more likely to get things in perspective and to remember that God absorbed our sins on the cross. Christians should first 'take it to the Lord in prayer'. (A good example of this is Psalm 73.) We feel indignation at injustice, but we do well to remember that perfect justice will not exist in this world and that God is the just Judge. Psalm 4:4 (quoted in Ephesians 4) first counsels that we should meditate and be still.

Then we can turn and talk to our brother or sister with a healthier sense of perspective.

2. Work on practical ways to dissipate your anger

- Don't feed your anger; starve it! In other words, don't let it fester and ferment beneath the surface.
- Direct anger appropriately. Yes, do take it out on a tennis ball (or a high-adrenaline activity of your choice). It is good to get the heart beating faster from physical exertion. But do also realize that the best displacement is to be found not in rage (even at a ball), but in the Lord. He alone is able to absorb / dissipate it, and he has 'borne our griefs, and carried our sorrows' (Isaiah 53:4, KJV).
- Consider driving or walking around the block before you walk in through the door after work. This will enable you to 'file away' the busyness of the day. You will be better able to transition into domestic life if you have a buffer between work and home (though the practicalities of this will vary, of course, according to the nature and place of your work).
- Make sure you get enough sleep: grumpiness and tiredness are often inextricable!

- Try to work back to the source of your anger. Is it general, brought on by the frustrations of life? Or is there a specific cause that can be addressed?
- Disagree with spoken words if you need to, but do so in the context of relationships. Doing this face to face, sitting down and apart from others (or with an impartial third party) is helpful.
- Always try seeing yourself from another person's perspective. For most of us, this does not come naturally.

3. Practise repentance and forgiveness

- Talking to yourself may, in fact, be a sign of sanity; in this context, it involves repeating biblical truths to yourself in order that these may shape your thoughts and actions. This is a good spiritual discipline.
- Remember that sin leaves your body through your mouth. 'If we claim to be without sin, we deceive ourselves and the truth is not in us. If we confess our sins, he is faithful and just and will forgive us our sins and purify us from all unrighteousness' (1 John 1:8–9).
- Sin can be:
  - **suppressed** or **repressed** (both Sigmund Freud and Romans 1:18–19 believe this to be unhealthy);
  - **expressed**, which might make us feel better initially, but ultimately leaves bitterness and hurt; or
  - **confessed**, which is the biblical way. The confession should be directed first to God, and then to others against whom we may have sinned.[18]
- Christian counsellors wisely advise that anger is best dissipated by forgiving the offender. Not only is this right

and clearly taught in the Bible, but it also releases us from self-justification and bitterness. None of this is easy, of course, particularly when the hurt runs deep, and getting the help of wise friends, pastors or a counsellor might be necessary.

This theme was consistently referred to during tributes at the state funeral of Nelson Mandela on 15 December 2013: despite the terrible injustices that he endured, he responded with forgiveness and refused to allow bitterness to fester.

The topic of anger is clearly bigger than the scope of this short chapter. However, my intention has been to summarize a biblical approach and provide some practical relief for anger-induced stress. It is my firm belief that dealing with the root cause of anger will do much to relieve the symptoms of stress in today's world.

 ## Getting personal

Thomas, it seems to me, is an angry man. This is evidenced in his mood swings and the verbal lashings he gives to family and colleagues. Maybe he had a bad childhood? Maybe he is frustrated by not attaining the career he had hoped for? Perhaps his marriage isn't what he expected? Maybe all of the above are issues for him. I hope that he will bring these things before the Lord, and own up to and confess his anger, first to himself, then to God, and ultimately to others.

I am concerned that **Susan** too needs to be careful in this area. Does she feel robbed of her children's childhood? Even though she has greatly reduced her morning commute, it is still very easy to bring home the aggression and frustration of each day and find it spilling over into family life. Finding space to connect well with her husband and her Lord is important to ensure that she too does not 'swallow dynamite'.

7. Be ambitious, but for the right reasons

I had a fortunate upbringing and a largely happy childhood. The island of Jersey was a great place to grow up on. And the sea was one of my two main loves.

The sea

I have already mentioned the influence of the sea in chapter 2: my summers were spent fishing, digging bait, swimming, sailing, walking the cliff tops, passing hours on the beach, watching waves crash in at high tide and pottering around the low water mark.

I loved – and still love – being around the sea. I now live the furthest away from the sea that I ever have, yet still I need to get regular sight of it to calm my heart and gain a sense of perspective. I am not alone in this regard.[1]

My ambition in life, as a teenager, was to be either a beach bum (which I guess is not much of an ambition!) or a professional rod fisherman. Neither of these held much prospect of fortune or fame.

The sight of the sea inculcates a sense of awe and reverence. The ocean is powerful, vast, unchanging, predictable, yet somehow different every day. Eventually, I came to realize that I couldn't live for the sea, because it points to something greater and beyond itself. The sea opened my eyes to a God who must have made all the oceans and who is even greater than them. He is a God who is powerful, vast, unchanging, and yet whose blessings are new every morning; great is his faithfulness (see Lamentations 3:22–23).

Music

My second passion in life was music. I started learning the piano when I was about six years old. Surprisingly, perhaps, most of the time I enjoyed practising! I also sang in the church choir.

The church that my family and I attended did not do much for me spiritually, and becoming a Christian almost necessarily involved moving away from it and attending somewhere else. In the worship services at my first church, it seemed to me, we rarely connected with God. There was a vague sense of awe and mystery around the communion table, but the vicar's sermons were unmemorable. I did not notice congregation members going away uplifted, appearing to believe, 'God is great and I really want to live for him.'

However, I do remember some very powerful existential moments to do with music and church. Cycling back from choir practice on Friday nights, I was often overcome with a real sense of reverence and wonder. God was big and vast and worthy of worship and praise. Music helped me to connect with this great truth.

I distinctly remember experiencing a great sense of awe as we sang the Charles Wesley hymn:

O for a heart to praise my God
A heart from sin set free
A heart that always feels thy blood
So freely shed for me.

It lifted my spirits to think that there really was a great big God 'out there', a God who made this world. 'Yes,' I thought, 'though I am a small dot in this vast universe, I have some worth, some significance, because God gave me life to enjoy.'

I have mentioned the sort of 'existential wonder' side of it. But there was also another part of my love for music which was private, leading me to retreat into myself and to develop a rather escapist outlook on life. As far as I was concerned, 'god' was all about me finding personal fulfilment in life.

My love of the created world, in particular the sea, and my love of music gave me reasons for living.

What we really, really want?

If we are going to live a full life, not overburdening it with stress, we will need to work out what we really want to live for.

British holidaymakers often go to Spain, enjoy the sea and the sun, have a wonderful time, return from holiday and promptly make plans to move back there as ex pats, because the lifestyle appears so enticing. Generally speaking, this is a mistake.[2] To turn a good leisure activity into a meaning for living usually doesn't work. We might wish to live life as if we were permanently on holiday, but in reality, we need to work. We need focused ambition and a sense of achievement in order to motivate us and give us meaning in life.

I hold the sea in great awe, but I don't live for it any more. Enjoyment of the created world is not intended to be a purpose for living, but rather a signpost beyond itself to the Creator God (see Psalm 19, for example). How much greater wonder there is in Jesus Christ: 'In him was life, and that life was the light of all mankind' (John 1:4). Jesus is the source of all life and light. He too is the One who can give us a quality existence with meaning and purpose.

My two loves, the sea and music, brought about a kind of hunger for God, which throughout my teenage years ached away inside me. I was never fully satisfied until God became the chief object of my love and my reason for living.

A life-verse

Do you have a verse that, for you, encapsulates your motivation for Christian living? In my case, it is Philippians 1:21: 'For to me, to live is Christ and to die is gain.'

This text of just ten words has come to be a life focus for me. The truth that it encapsulates has helped me enormously as I've sought to put the challenges and stresses of life in their biblical perspective. It truly does contain the meaning of life.

'For me to live – really live – is . . .' What would you put in there? What do you really live for? What energizes you and makes you feel most alive?

It wasn't until the sixth form at school that I met up with other teenage Christians. They took me to the Christian Union, and then I joined a Friday night group called 'Youthquake', where the initial attraction was that girls outnumbered boys six to one! But I also remember the vicar's patience there in answering the many questions about the Christian faith.

I do not actually remember the time, place or date when I became a Christian. But what I do remember is that this existence completely reoriented my priorities. Up to this point, I had had no real idea of what I wanted to do with my life. I had had no incentive for studying and had already done very badly in my O levels. Now, it seemed, there was a motivation to work hard. I now had an ambition to achieve, which included a new appetite for study.

Becoming a Christian was all about meeting the living Jesus. He was now real to me, closer than a friend, and knowing him gave meaning and purpose to my life.

As I look back and reflect on my Christian beginnings, I notice that becoming a Christian reoriented me from a slightly introspective outlook on life to one where I wanted to be in a community. No-one had to tell me to go to church or Bible study – I could not get enough of them. I am not sure whether your core personality can alter, but becoming a Christian made me more aware of other people and more concerned for their welfare.

I had no separate 'call to ministry'. I think I just assumed that if you were a Christian, then you could want to be in this business full-time. I could think of no other life I wanted to live . . . this was worth everything to me.

That is as far as I will go with my personal story, because what happened leading up to that point and my conversion is what guided me to that central purpose for life. Philippians 1:21 became my focus and my life-verse, and that desire has stayed with me ever since.

Yes, for me to live, to really live, is Christ. Yes, I still love the sea and music, but to *live* is Christ . . .

To live is Christ

Commentaries on Philippians 1:21 devote space to exploring whether Paul is talking about the physicality of human life (he gives us breath and numbers our days on earth), or whether his focus is on spiritual realities (primarily about new life in Christ).

When we read the context of Philippians chapter 1, it seems clear that Paul certainly intends us to understand verse 21 as meaning: 'I owe my physical life and existence to Christ.' When I die, I will go to be with him, leaving behind this ageing, frail body and entering my eternal, heavenly home.

Paul writes this letter from prison and in chains, probably in Rome. The prospect of death is near. He contemplates deliverance (v. 19) and prays that he may experience it, but if not, that he may have courage in death, and that by both his life and his death Christ may be exalted.

I wonder whether we, in the modern world, have forgotten the stark reality separating life and death. The way in which people die is very different from that of a previous generation. People often die in hospital with morphine drips and nursing care, but away from family and friends. And, of course, our culture persuades us to do everything we can to prevent ourselves from getting (or at least looking) old – from colouring our hair and applying anti-wrinkle cream, to face lifts and tummy tucks.

My trips to Africa frequently remind me how apparently more expendable and fragile life there is, and, perhaps because death is all around, it is spoken of more openly. Death is painful, and people often do not just 'slip away'.

And yet, Paul may mean more than: 'God gives me physical life and strength.' For him, to live is Christ. This is what he lives for. And this seems to imply that he means 'life' in terms of a qualitative life. This would echo Jesus' words: 'I have come that you might have life in all its fullness' (John 10:10). Paul, of course, is not implying that he expected to live 100 or 200 years, but rather that life with Jesus is a quality of living that outside of him Paul could never know.

The primary meaning of this text then is: the reason for our existence is life in God, and when you exist in that way, you really do live. That is why Philippians 1:21 is my favourite text.

To die is gain

However, my passion for Philippians 1:21 is subject to some mockery from my wife: 'You're just a typical man – you only talk about death being "gain" because you are desperate to get out of your chores and pop off to heaven . . . and no doubt leave me to get on with everything while you shirk your responsibilities. And, anyway, how can you think of death as "gain" when you will leave behind our lovely children and family?' To preach this text as escapism would of course be a mistake. So, over the years, I have mustered my defence, not least by observing the balance of the text:

For me to live is Christ; *and*

To die is gain

Depending on our individual temperaments, we may well place emphasis on one or other aspect of the text:

- 'In Christ, in this life, we have fullness of joy, purpose and meaning for living' – how sad when it all ends. This is a joy-filled letter, and Paul wants his joy (v. 18) to be their joy (v. 26).
- 'Heaven is so much more than "pie in the sky"; there is eternity with God. I do not want to make my home in this world; I should be "homesick for heaven". So, I will make sure that in everything I do, my ultimate focus is on my final destination.'

I think Paul says both:

- If he remains on earth, it will mean fruitful labour
  (v. 22). Paul was a highly ambitious man with a desire
  to see the whole world won for Christ. Even as death
  approached, he was making plans. He says, 'I know that
  I will remain, and I will continue with all of you for
  your progress and joy in the faith, so that through my
  being with you again your boasting in Christ Jesus will
  abound on account of me' (Philippians 1:25–26).
- But he really desires to depart and be with Christ, to be
  at home in heaven with him (v. 23). He is genuinely
  torn. Not because he is an escapist, but because he has
  a tangible sense that to go home is to be with Christ,
  forever.

This text is true. In many respects, the verse is not difficult to understand. If you are convinced that Jesus Christ is your life and yet you remain living in a highly stressful world, what are the implications for you? How can this verse be true for you? Philippians 1:21 is a very personal text: Paul says, for *me* to live is Christ, and what a contrast this is to his previous motivation! (See Philippians 3:4–6.)

What gets you out of bed?

I can remember a school Christian Union meeting I attended soon after becoming a Christian. The visiting speaker had completed his talk and opened up the meeting for questions. I am sure that he expected some of the typical apologetic questions that had exercised the students in recent meetings: 'What is the meaning of suffering?'; 'Why are there so many religions?'; 'Why did Jesus come?'; 'If God exists, why are there atheists?', for example. But the question one of our sixth formers asked was: 'What makes you get out of bed in the morning?' Perhaps not that surprising a question for a teenager to ask! Nevertheless, it is still a good question. What motivates you to live?

Some people get out of bed:

- to make money
- to build homes
- to raise children
- to further their careers or be famous.

None of these things is wrong in themselves, but unless it is Jesus who gets you out of bed, you haven't yet learned: 'for me to live is Christ'. American pastor Mark Driscoll makes the point well: 'When you have a little picture of Jesus, your problems get bigger. When you have a big picture of Jesus, your problems get smaller because you see them under the lordship, under the rule, under the dominion of Jesus.'[3]

What is your reason for living, and indeed your reason for dying? Having a clear answer to this question will determine the whole focus of your life.

A different perspective on death

For many people, to die is a wasted life, a tragic loss, the end of hope.

I have taken some very sad funerals in my time as vicar, where family and friends appear to make a tremendous effort to give the deceased a great send-off, but with no hope of heaven or life beyond.

In a cemetery in England, you can read these words on the tombstone:

> Remember man, as you walk by, As you are now, so once was I,
> As I am now, so shall you be, Remember this and follow me.

To which someone replied by writing on the tombstone:

> To follow you I'll not consent, Until I know which way you
> went.[4]

Apparently, on his deathbed Oscar Wilde said, 'Either that wallpaper goes or I do', and then died!

The film director, Woody Allen, has addressed the complexities and pain of modern living in many of his films. He once observed, 'I don't mind dying; I just don't want to be around when it happens.' Elsewhere he said, 'I don't want to achieve immortality through my work; I want to achieve it by not dying.'

Witty, but also tragic.

Paul had a different perspective on death. He was obviously genuinely torn: why would he want to remain in this life when heaven awaits? There he will see Jesus face to face! There he will be free of this body of sin! There we will enjoy pleasures forever at the right hand of God.

And yet, because he is confident about the eternal destination and knows that his final home is secure, while on this earth, he says, 'I will labour fruitfully.' He is not just sitting in the departure lounge waiting for his final flight home. This is Paul's expectation for his remaining life on earth:

- 'Fruitful labour'. Fruit takes time, and tending a fruit-bearing tree requires labour; he will work for the good fruit to be borne in the Philippians' lives (v. 22).
- [It is] 'necessary that I remain'. He has a sense of call, a sense of purpose for being here, to work to God's agenda for his people (v. 24).

- '. . . for your progress and joy'. He is concerned that his remaining time is for the benefit of God's people (v. 25).

Paul played to win

Paul says:

- 'I press on towards the goal to win the prize for which God has called me heavenwards in Christ Jesus' (Philippians 3:14).
- 'Run in such a way as to get the prize' (1 Corinthians 9:24b).

Every two years, the Isthmian games came to Corinth. Paul could well have been in town as the games were going on in AD 51 and have had them in mind when he wrote his first letter to the Corinthian church. Although not quite as big as the modern Olympics, they nevertheless captivated the town and were the climax of years of preparation and training. There were six main events: racing, wrestling, boxing, jumping, discus throwing and javelin throwing. When Paul saw all the excitement and hype surrounding the games, he encouraged the Corinthians to be that enthusiastic about the message about Jesus Christ.

Yes, I would be a Christian for the fullness of life that it gives now, but if there is no heaven, then this life is futile. Paul says something similar in 1 Corinthians 15:12–19.

Paul is not directionless, neither is he without purpose. However, his ambition is directed towards long-term, not short-term goals. He has his eyes focused on the finishing line. His drive, discipline and ambition resonate with modern competitiveness. And yet, stressed people today would also do well to learn from the fact that this life is fleeting, often full of troubles and only reaching its full climax at the end.

Paul is like his master who 'for the sake of the joy that was set before him endured the cross' (Hebrews 12:2).

There is a crown that will last forever, and it is worth whatever sacrifices it takes to make sure that we are rewarded in the end. The rewards of the Christian life are mainly in the future.

Life: a gift to be spent

If we imbibe Paul's attitude, we will find that this frees us up to 'spend' life and work for the things that are life-giving. As the popular sentiment says, life should be lived to the full. But life is also short. It would be a terrible shame to get to the end of this life and regret our investment of time, money and energy.

Spend life wisely!

The wisdom of the psalmist still holds true: 'The days of our years are threescore years and ten; and if by reason of strength they be fourscore years, yet is their strength labour and sorrow; for it is soon cut off, and we fly away' (Psalm 90:10, KJV). For all our modern medicine, we have hardly changed that in nearly 2,500 years.

Because Jesus Christ is Paul's 'all' and his final destiny is secure in Christ, Paul has an attitude to life that enables him to take risks. C. T. Studd expressed a similar sentiment when he said, 'If Jesus Christ be God and died for me, then no sacrifice can be too great for me to make for him.'[5]

It is easy to lose this biblical perspective. All too often, we hold on for dear life to this world, and barely give the life after it a second thought.

Striving with a godly ambition

Imagine an eight-year-old boy kicking a football in a side street in Manchester. An expensive car pulls up, and the man in the rear seat winds down his window to speak to him. The passenger turns out to be the Manager of Manchester United Football Club. He spends a moment watching the boy kick the ball and then says to him, 'Son, when you are 18, I will sign you up and you will play for Manchester United. I can guarantee that.'

Every boy's dream has just come true! That lad would be so excited. He has been promised a secure place in the squad. What effect would this have upon him? If he takes the man at his word, then he can be sure of a place on the team. He might as well hang up his boots and wait ten years. Really? Is that likely to be the effect of the manager's promise? I think not. More likely, *because* the boy has a place on the squad, he will train his hardest, making sure that he is match-fit and in tip-top condition for his first game with the team.

This illustration helps put ambition in its proper place. Ambition can drive you to succeed, always striving to be the best, making you restless and unsatisfied. But ambition can also make you seek to be your very best because already you are secure in your relationship with God and seeking his glory in all things.

Paul reflects something of this godly ambition: 'by the grace of God I am what I am, and his grace to me was not without effect. No, I worked harder than all of them – yet not I, but the grace of God that was with me' (1 Corinthians 15:10).

Alister Chapman's sympathetic assessment of the life of the late Revd Dr John Stott, *Godly Ambition*, is well worth a read. Chapman seeks to unpack Stott's desire for humility and ambition for Christ's sake to co-exist:

. . . the difficulty in practice of course is that godly ambition
and selfish ambition were sometimes hard to tell apart . . .
[this book] is a critical yet sympathetic account of a gifted and
determined man who wanted to do all he could to further
God's kingdom and became a Christian star in the process.
It is a story of godly ambition . . .[6]

Conclusion

As Rick Warren would remind us in his best-selling book,
we need to have a 'purpose-driven life'. But will you make
your purpose in life the glory of God?[7] Will you allow
yourself to be spent for his purposes? In our striving for
balance and rest (see the next chapter), we should remember that life is a gift to be spent and, ultimately, rest is for
heaven.

Don't play it safe, risk-free and comfortable. It is not possible
to live a risk-free life, but the risks can and should be calculated
on the basis of glorifying God and living life for him. Will you
pray for boldness to live a life for him and in due course die a
death that glorifies him?

 Getting personal

Both **Susan** and **Anna** are purposeful – and thus manage
to achieve an enormous amount in their busy lives. As
Susan changes her pace of life a bit, continues to retrain
in her new career and seeks to get her life into better
proportion, I hope very much that she will make Christ
her first love. The only true meaning for living will be
found in focusing on him.

To **Jack**, I want to say, ambition is not bad. There is a danger that, with his laid-back personality, he does not see his life as being purposeful. He might need to be more proactive in relationships with his family members. He also needs to plan for his future, more so than might come naturally to him. Does he have a pension plan? Has he budgeted for family expenditure? Will he allow himself to be pushed outside of his comfort zone and engage actively in his family's life? This will all be a challenge for him, but it will be essential if he is not to frustrate and overburden those around him. In return, I am completely confident that Martha will respect and love him all the more for any sign of proactivity.

Do you know any 'Jacks'? How would you pray for/ advise them, in the light of this chapter's teaching?

8. Work, rest and worship

My first car was an old Renault 16, which I bought cheaply off my sister. I was still a teenager, rather prone to over-confidence and possessing little wisdom. My father warned me, 'Remember, it is called a speed limit, not a target.' He added, 'She [the car] is an old lady who does not want to be driven at full stretch.'

Of course, such wisdom is likely to fall on deaf ears. It was only after I had wrapped this particular car around a granite wall at the bottom of St Aubin's Hill on a slippery night that my driving moderated a little. On a recent visit to Jersey, some thirty years later, I checked, and the wall is still just fine!

We live life in a rush:

- We keep packed diaries and fill up every minute of the day, often failing to include in our schedules eating, sleeping and exercising.

- We check email constantly, tweet our every movement, check in with Facebook, talk on the phone. Social media becomes a nervous habit.[1]
- We complain we are tired, but we don't actively take time out to allow our body, mind, emotions and spirit to recover.
- If we get ill, we soldier on without taking time off.
- At other times, we know we need rest and relaxation, but do not take it, because we feel it will be a waste of time or others will assume us to be lazy.
- Often we are in need of real rest, but feel guilty about 'not doing anything'.
- Alternatively, we seek to rest but we are too restless to enjoy our time off.
- Even when we retire, we say to people, 'I'm just as busy now as I was before – in fact, I don't know how I ever found time to go to work!'

I recognize all of this in me. I also know that my productivity decreases if I am over-busy. But I do need some work, some pressure, in order to be productive.

I have noticed that without adequate challenge in my day, I can fritter away my time surfing the internet, skimming books or pouring yet another cup of coffee. But if I experience too much pressure, I will fail to complete tasks adequately and I will feel out of control.

In a nutshell, the biblical advice is the 'six out of seven principle'. Labour for six; rest for one.

The Ten Commandments are full of 'thou shalt not', but the fourth commandment is one of only two positive instructions: 'Remember the Sabbath day by keeping it holy . . .' This commandment is not as clear as it at first seems, however. For the modern reader, it raises a number of questions.

Work: What is meant by work? We are not subsistence labourers, and we live in a world which appears never to sleep. How does this principle apply to twenty-first-century living?

Rest: What is meant by rest, ceasing from our labours? Many people have reacted against an overly prescriptive Christian legalism which forbad certain activities on Sunday. But the question remains: 'Should a Christian cease from labour one day per week for worship and rest?'

Worship: What is meant by a 'holy day'? This is the notion behind the word 'holiday'. Does this principle apply to modern Christians? Is the purpose of this day 'rest' or 'worship'?

Let us look at each of these in turn.

Work, rest and worship – in biblical perspective

1. Work is a gift from God, not a curse

Work-related stress is a huge problem, exacerbated by factors we have previously mentioned (email, social media, global connectivity and unrealistic expectations). But too little work or unemployment creates its own stress in the form of boredom, anxiety and feelings of worthlessness.

When life seems overwhelming and work is drudgery, it is helpful for me to remember that we worship a 'working God'.

Genesis 1 – 2 shows us that God was at work bringing this world into being and that he continues to sustain it even to this day. It is in this context that the Sabbath-day principle was first instituted. For six days, God laboured, and on the seventh day, he rested. Bible commentators agree that this does not mean that God ceased working (for otherwise this world would spin off its axis), but rather that he transitioned from 'creating' to 'sustaining' and enjoying that which he had made. Each new day is a gift from God and, in a real sense, a new creation.

We note in Genesis 1 – 2 that Adam and Eve worked the garden and enjoyed the fruit of God's creation. It is a mistake to think that work itself is the judgment of God. What happened after the Fall was that work became *toil* (see Genesis 3:17–19).

Work is good, but toil is draining. This helps explain why we have such a love / hate relationship with work. We want to do it, but it is burdensome.

Often I hate working, and feel loath to turn up on a Monday morning. But I also hate *not* working and find that even when I have time for vacation and relaxation, I discover myself looking for work. My identity and self-worth are tied up with work in some way.

Working in the modern world needs some redefinition to encompass the things we do that are not rest. While the creation principle is six days of labour and one day of rest, the average working week tends to be five days followed by a weekend off. Some amplification of our definitions is required.

So, what is work?

Work – wider than employment, and not just done by the paid

I think most people would agree that work is not just the hours spent at a factory or a desk from 9am to 5pm. 'Work' should describe everything we do to provide for our living. It at least encompasses activities such as gardening, shopping, house-work, 'fixing things', or the time spent answering email messages on a smartphone on the train home. The list is long.

Students, stay-at-home parents, the unemployed and the retired all work, even if they do not bring home a salary.

In short, work is good but it needs careful defining in our day and age.

2. Rest is not a luxury but a necessity

Living by the Sabbath principle

While the Bible warns against idleness, it also offers great wisdom on the business of 'work, rest and play', not least, the requirement of one day's rest after six days of labour. This too, like the speed limit, is not a target. Although most people in the modern world would do well to keep *at least* one day in seven as rest.

The late Verna Wright was Professor of Rheumatology at Leeds University and a consultant advisor to the Department of Health and Social Security. He commented on the wisdom of this seven-day cycle: God provides a day of rest to combat the harmful effects of a week of stress.[2] Like many of the things that we have observed so far in this book, knowing them is only half the battle. Changing our lifestyle to live in line with what we think is good for us is quite another thing.

I hope to persuade you that the Sabbath principle should still shape modern living. But more than that, I also hope that I can help you see that the need for rest and recreation is not an idle escape from life, but rather it is a necessity if we are to live productive lives in a stressful world. Hence:

> Remember the Sabbath day by keeping it holy. Six days you shall labour and do all your work, but the seventh day is a Sabbath to the LORD your God. On it you shall not do any work, neither you, nor your son or daughter, nor your male or female servant, nor your animals, nor any foreigner residing in your towns. For in six days the LORD made the heavens and the earth, the sea, and all that is in them, but he rested on the seventh day. Therefore the LORD blessed the Sabbath day and made it holy.
>
> (Exodus 20:8–11)

Sir James Crichton-Browne said,

> We doctors, in the treatment of nervous diseases, are now
> constantly compelled to prescribe periods of rest. Some
> periods are, I think, only Sundays in arrears.[3]

The pressures we all feel in a busy world are often exacerbated
by our expectations of one another within the church. For
many churchgoers, Sundays are not a day of rest. Even
midweek, we may rush from one meeting to another and
commend one another for our Christian busyness. Ambition
can be good, we agree, but stress-inducing busyness seems to
miss out on the biblical principle.

Rest – life has rhythm and purpose

After the French Revolution, the Republic changed the
calendar and introduced a ten-day week in 1792. The decision
was in part designed to break from the various Christian
calendars. There were now twelve months, each divided into
three ten-day weeks called *décades*. Each day was divided
into ten hours of a hundred minutes of a hundred seconds –
exactly 100,000 seconds per day.

Thirteen years later, the experiment was abandoned.
Workers complained that a ten-day working week gave less
rest (one day off in ten rather than one in seven) and because
it broke with rhythms that had long been recognized by many
different nations and cultures.

At the beginning of the twentieth century, various experiments were undertaken in Russia to depart from the Gregorian
calendar in favour of the Soviet calendar, for similar reasons.
Motivated by Communist ideals such as workforce productivity and the elimination of religious observance, they tried
six-day working weeks, with factories operating 24 hours per

day. The scheme was called the 'continuous production week'. Experiments ceased in 1940, with a return to the traditional pattern of Sunday as a day off in a cycle of a seven-day week.

Verna Wright's further observations on this point are helpful:

> [I have] observed that just as the body requires its 24-hour cycle, so the one in 7 rest day fits perfectly the needs of the body and mind . . . Speaking as a physician, there are good reasons physically, mentally and spiritually why we should set aside the first day of the week as a special day unto the Lord.[4]

As the French and Soviet experiments would seem to confirm, a rhythm of Sabbath rest is not there just for the good of Christian believers. The biblical pattern for work and rest is good for all humanity and is therefore an ordinance from creation:

> By the seventh day God had finished the work he had been doing; so on the seventh day he rested from all his work. Then God blessed the seventh day and made it holy, because on it he rested from all the work of creating that he had done.
> (Genesis 2:2–3)

The text of Genesis 2 states that God did not just take the Sabbath off and then go back to work again. Rather, it implies that God entered into a period of rest, not one of inactivity but a period where God now enjoyed the fruit of his labour. In the New Testament, Jesus assumed that healing on the Sabbath day was not breaking the fourth commandment because 'doing good' and 'saving life' were more important than a Pharisaic observance (see Mark 3:1–6).

There is much wisdom here for those of us dealing with stress in the modern world: we might deduce from this that the goal of one day off in seven is to help make sense of the work of the other six, to pause to consider our Creator who has given us a world in which to work and be fruitful, to enjoy some of the fruits of our labour, and to anticipate the eternal rest where God dwells. The author of Hebrews (see Hebrews chapter 4) makes precisely these points: the goal of our life is to enter into the promised rest (that is, heaven). This alone can make sense of the work and toil of this life. The promised rest, ultimately, is not the Sabbath, or Sunday, but entering into the eternal rest of heaven.

Sleep deprivation as a method of torture has been success-fully used.[5] There is also evidence that 'deep sleep' (REM or rapid-eye-movement sleep) is the time when our brains file away the worries and stresses of the day, enabling us to wake up refreshed and ready for more mental challenges.

Rest requires recuperation and relaxation. The Greek scholar Archimedes reportedly shouted, 'Eureka!' (meaning 'I have found it' in ancient Greek) from his bath as he noticed the impact of water displacement. The eureka moment has come to epitomize the moment of clarity which often comes when we walk away from our desk and all of a sudden discover that a problem is solved in our mind and the way ahead is clear. Yes, intense concentration and focus are required, but often the 'fix' is not there until we break from our labours for a while. Remember the wise words from earlier in this book that someone shared with me: 'You need to do something in life which means that you don't think about work or other problems while you are doing it.' For some, that is a round of golf, for others a trek up a 3,000-foot mountain. These moments away from our labours are required for greater productivity. Find time to do whatever works for you.

Time away from work is not wasted time
God's provision of manna in the wilderness, mentioned in chapter 5 of this book, is a perfect illustration of the above (see Exodus 16:4–5). God provided for the children of Israel on a daily basis. Every day, they needed to collect a fresh supply, except on the evening before the Sabbath when they collected double the amount, and on the following day the manna was still good to eat. Not working is not a waste. We pray, 'Give us today our daily bread.' We can't stockpile, and we can trust God to supply even when we observe the Sabbath principle of rest.

A modern example is to be found in the fast-food chain Chick-fil-A. This is the only major fast-food restaurant chain to continue to close on Sundays, even though this is one of the busiest days of the week for restaurateurs. Despite this apparent disadvantage, for forty consecutive years, sales have increased over a six-day (rather than seven-day) working week. S. Truett Cathy says,

> I was not so committed to financial success that I was willing to abandon my principles and priorities. One of the most visible examples of this is our decision to close on Sunday. Our decision to close on Sunday was our way of honouring God and of directing our attention to things that mattered more than our business.[6]

God has put order and rhythm into every human being. This requires that we give our body time out to rest and enjoy the fruit of our labour.

A Sabbath for all?
A day of rest is not just about preserving Sunday worship for Christians. In fact, the way in which the Ten Commandments are framed indicates that rest is needed for people of all faiths

and none. It would seem that the principles of rest and rhythm, outlined above, are good for all human beings because of the way we are made.

Nevertheless, a careful look at the two places in the Bible that record the giving of the Ten Commandments will yield further insights into the purpose of the Sabbath. In both instances, the people are instructed to keep the Sabbath day holy, but the motivation for Sabbath observance differs.

Exodus 20:11 states, 'For in six days the LORD made the heavens and the earth, the sea, and all that is in them, but he rested on the seventh day. Therefore the LORD blessed the Sabbath day and made it holy.'

Deuteronomy 5:15 states, 'Remember that you were slaves in Egypt and that the LORD your God brought you out of there with a mighty hand and an outstretched arm. Therefore the LORD your God has commanded you to observe the Sabbath day.'

The Exodus account of the commandments emphasizes the 'creation ordinance' outlined above. The Deuteronomy account reminds the people of Israel of their rescue from slavery.

3. Worship: man's chief end is to glorify God

For the early church, worship patterns were complex. Initially, they kept the Sabbath, as did all the other Jews. On the first day of the week (the Sunday), presumably after work, they met together to worship God and share in the Lord's Supper. In time, and certainly post Emperor Constantine, for most Christians, Sunday became the day of Sabbath.

Since then, Christians have looked upon Sunday as a special day to be reverenced, because Jesus rose on that day from the dead. Sunday celebrates our day of redemption and rescue from the slavery of sin. However, although the Sabbath principle remains, its application has altered.

Sabbath observance is necessary for our sanctification. God made it a 'holy day' in order that we might stand out as different and testify to the world about God's creative and redeeming goodness. Question one of the Westminster Shorter Catechism summarizes this combination of enjoyment and obedience: 'the chief end of man is to glorify God and enjoy him forever.'

Principles for observing the Sabbath in a stress-filled modern world

1. The Sabbath exhorts rest for all people and worship for God's people

I am persuaded that we can no longer legislate for a special Sunday observance, not least because in a multicultural society, the Jew is likely to want that to be a Saturday, the Moslem a Friday, and so on. As part of a Christian minority, I am not sure that we can do any more than ask for freedom to worship God on the Sunday.

Having said this, the dilemma is that without an overriding religious conviction, the nation no longer has a 'corporate' day off, the land never rests and the country never goes silent. Needless to say, none of this helps stress!

I believe that we should work towards freedom of religious practice for all. My employer should not stop me from worshipping God.

I also believe that we should do all we can to allow God's creation principles to be expressed in one day of rest per six days of labour. Tim Keller makes the point well:

God ties the Sabbath to freedom from slavery. Anyone who overworks is really a slave. Anyone who cannot rest from work is a slave – to a need for success, to a materialistic culture, to exploitative employers, to parental expectations, or to all of the above. These slave masters will abuse you if you are not disciplined in the practice of Sabbath rest. Sabbath is a declaration of freedom.[7]

2. The Sabbath requires a careful definition of work and rest

We have already noted two principles. Work is wider than paid employment, and work is good, but full of toil.

With these principles in mind, then our rest also needs to be appropriate. To use trivial examples:

- If I am a lifeguard, then I am unlikely to go swimming on my day off, and I may instead want to sit down with a good book.
- If I am a librarian, then sitting down with a good book may be the last thing I will want to do, but going for a swim may be just the thing to provide me with needful rest.

It is important that you 'know yourself'. Are you rejuvenated by rigorous exercise or by curling up by a log fire with a book? Do you crave company or prefer a few hours of solitude?

Our Sabbath is a day to enjoy the fruit of our labour. It is a day to have a break from toil. It is a day to spend worshipping God, and, incidentally, I wonder whether one hour in the morning at church was quite what God had in mind. A Victorian work ethic made Sabbath observance so dull. But in our day, we are in danger of treating our Sabbath day like every other day.

The surprising thing is that observing the God-given rhythm of rest is also the key to true productivity. When Paul wrote of 'redeeming the time' (Ephesians 5:16, KJV), in part I believe he meant that by living our lives according the Maker's instructions, we 'buy back the time' and make it useful for God.

3. The Sabbath reminds us that we are made for worship

We are to be a 'holy' people. This means that our approach to work, worship, rest and play should be different. This is not just about being separate from the world or excluding ourselves from the world (the Amish way?). The positive emphasis on holiness is that of being separated *for* God: setting aside time, energy and gifts to be with him.

There should be much about the Christian outlook that will be attractive to the non-believing culture. Should we not be modelling life in all its fullness? Enjoying God and enjoying God's world?

Augustine wrote these well-known words: 'You have made us for yourself, O Lord, and our heart is restless until it rests in you.'[8]

More than a thousand years later, the great Victorian statesman William Gladstone said, 'Tell me what the young men of England are doing on Sunday, and I will tell you what the future of England will be.'

I wonder what he would make of our young men and women today?

A journalist from the *Chicago Tribune* observed,

One weekend, recently, I looked out the window and discovered that Sunday had disappeared. Nobody had swiped it exactly, but something had gone out of the noble day. Suddenly, I realized what it was: Sunday had turned into Tuesday. Out on the street, people no longer were strolling about. They had direction, a midweek glint in their eyes that

meant business. They were walking briskly in and out of
stores instead of browsing quietly past the windows. The
scene was as busy as your average workaday Tuesday,
throwing the whole week out of whack.

Now Sunday is just another day, and it appears to have lost
its real purpose. Back in the old days, Sunday had character.
It was prim, but underneath it had a certain toughness. It was
the most sturdy and unflappable of days, one people could
count on. You did not market; you did not go to the office for
a few hours; you didn't even hunt for antiques. One of the
things you definitely did not do was go downtown and buy
sheets in a sale.

But just try lying around the house on Sunday now –
knowing that half the world is out there doing things. Even
people who claim to be relaxing are jogging and exercising like
mad. So you see, we truly do need Sunday back the way it was,
as a weekend cushion.[9]

We are a restless age. We are over-stimulated with visual and
audio input. We need to learn to rest.

Recently, I went for a walk in some glorious English
countryside. But my mind was racing and my eyes were
unable to take in the beauty in front of me. It wasn't until
several hours into the walk that I was able to settle my gaze
and see the world through fresh eyes.

Why do we speed down the motorway on our way to
holiday? Have you noticed that it takes time to unwind and
relax? Rest needs to be planned for in advance. Books have
introductions and conclusions, and symphonies have overtures
and finales. Life too needs 'margins'. In a stressful world, the
urgent will always squeeze out space and time to relax, unless
doing this is scheduled in advance. Rest will not be attained if
wind-down time is never achieved.

Remember the words of Jesus quoted in chapter 1? Take comfort in the great gift that Jesus offers:

> 'Come to me, all you who are weary and burdened, and I will give you rest. Take my yoke upon you and learn from me, for I am gentle and humble in heart, and you will find rest for your souls. For my yoke is easy and my burden is light.'
> (Matthew 11:28–30)

Jesus offers to swap burdens with us. Worshipping God is not necessarily inactivity. Rather it is taking off the wearisome burden of this life and placing it on Jesus' back, and then taking up his easy load and finding rest for our souls.

True worship is about being in tune with our Lord and Maker, and finding joy in his work. In his service there is perfect freedom.

Putting these principles into practice requires planning for:

- **work**: being productive and good stewards at work
- **rest**: we should not be working all the time. Take time off without feeling guilty
- **worship**: setting aside a Sabbath day of rest and making worship part of the rhythm of daily and weekly life.

 Getting personal

Susan has made some substantial changes to her life, and friends and family are starting to notice the difference. However, she finds it difficult to rest. The 'hurry' mentality is still part of her make-up. Even when she has some spare time, she looks for ways to fill it. She feels a little bored and rather guilty when she is not busy. She needs to learn that relaxation and Sabbath rest are not luxuries, but necessities. The world will keep spinning without her active intervention, and she does not need to be in control of everything. In her organized lifestyle, she needs to plan for rest: a relaxed meal with friends? A walk in the countryside? Time with siblings or friends that does not need military-level operational planning? Or could she even conceive of having a day where she has nothing planned? This might not come naturally to Susan, but she could learn it over time.

9. Joy and thankfulness as a way of life

Joy is invigorating! I can remember some very joyful occasions:

- My heart skipping a beat as I saw my bride walk down the aisle towards me twenty-five years ago.
- Trembling with excitement on the phone as I announced to the family the birth of our first baby.
- Joining the roar of the crowd from behind the goal line as the home team spectacularly scored a goal late into the second half.
- Feeling my heart pound within my chest during the last few steps to the summit of Ben Nevis as I took in the vista.
- Talking with feverish excitement as I landed my first (and only) bass, which weighed in at over 7lb.

Joy energizes and excites us. It gets the adrenaline pumping through the body. Living life to the full with a sense of purpose and gratitude – that is joy.

I also remember miserable days at the end of the breakwater in Jersey, desperately waiting for a bite on my fishing line. It was a popular place for holidaymakers to view the coast of France, and as they wandered by, their typical remark was: 'Any joy?' Good question!

Whether you are a bouncing Tigger, a reflective Pooh, a worrying Piglet or a morose Eeyore, joy needs to be part of your life if you are going to remove stress and enjoy your existence.[1]

As I write, the university term is starting up, and freshers' week is in full swing. Partying and clubbing before the slog of a new term begins. Is that joy? And is it meant to be so short-lived? I suspect that the world seeks fun, whereas the Bible promises joy. There is a subtle but profound difference: fun and happiness vary according to circumstances; joy is found through a relationship with God.

I have some sympathy with the lady's response to the cheery captain during a very rough sea crossing. 'Madam, do not worry,' he said. 'No-one has ever died from sea sickness.' 'Why would you say that?' she objected. 'It is only the hope of death that is keeping me going.'

While British people may often be characterized as unduly Eeyore-ish, the Tiggers of this world can be very irritating! Slowly recovering from post-viral illness in my early twenties, I found that there was nothing worse than hearing people tritely telling me to cheer up.

Defining joy

Remember that the answer to question one of the Westminster Shorter Catechism includes the idea of enjoying God forever? The Bible is clear: we are made for a joyful relationship with God, but sin separates us from joy.[2] The New Testament recognizes at least ten varieties of joy: exultant joy; optimism; gladness or good cheer; pleasure; hilarity; boasting; blessedness or happiness; leaping for joy; inward joy; shared joy.[3]

Joy is not about temperament, nor, as we have noticed, is it to do with having fun or being a bright, sunny personality. A melancholic Christian may experience Christian joy, and an extrovert non-Christian may not. Dr Martyn Lloyd-Jones, the great twentieth-century preacher, wrote,

> Temperament is a gift from God but as a result of the Fall, and of sin, temperament is to be kept in its place. It is a wonderful gift, but to be controlled . . . Our feelings are always seeking to control us, and unless we realize this, they will undoubtedly do so . . . Feelings must be engaged in true Christianity, but the mere fact that we have not had certain feelings does not of necessity mean that we are not Christian.[4]

Jonathan Edwards expressed it like this in one of his early resolutions:

> Resolved, to endeavour to obtain for myself as much happiness in the other world as I possibly can, with all the power, might, vigour and vehemence, yea, violence, I am capable of, or can bring myself to exert, in any way that can be thought of.[5]

Joy in spite of . . .

Dr Packer lists some of the joy-sapping experiences of Christians:

- four black 'D's' – disappointment, desolation, depression, desperation
- four black 'F's' – frustration, failure, fear, fury.

But we are not victims and prisoners of either the past or the present. 'Christians have, so to speak, larger souls than other people,' he says, 'for grief and joy, like desolation and hope, or pain and peace, can coexist in their lives in a way that non-Christians know nothing about.'[6]

Paul's most positive letter is the one to the Christians in Philippi. It is a letter full of joy, as Paul commands his hearers to 'rejoice in the Lord always' (Philippians 4:4).[7] By way of contrast, he asks the Galatians in exasperation: 'Where is your joy?' (Galatians 4:15). Like the apostle Paul, it is possible to be 'sorrowful yet always rejoicing' (2 Corinthians 6:10). This is a paradox of Christian experience. We can endure the gravity of life's circumstances and the reality of our human and spiritual position, and at the same time have joy.[8] Even the thought of martyrdom brings about joy (Philippians 1:19–26). This too was Jesus' joy, as Hebrews 12:2 affirms. Joy is anticipated now, as a foretaste of heaven. And because the joy of heaven will be so great, we may experience joy even when the Christian life is very difficult, for we know it is not deferred forever.

Joy, in general, is motivated by three things: We rejoice that Jesus came in the past (Luke 1:46–47), we rejoice in the present (1 Peter 1:6), and we rejoice in the future (Revelation 19:7). The 'happy' or 'blessed' man of the Beatitudes is the person who shares the joy of being a member of God's kingdom. This blessedness is associated particularly with the announcement of the kingdom of God. Why, even God himself loves a 'cheerful' giver (2 Corinthians 9:7). After all, a grudging and despondent attitude in giving is a poor response to the God who gave so much and so freely in Christ (2 Corinthians 9:15).

Words for 'joy'

Moving on from this general overview, two New Testament words are of particular interest.

Firstly, *hēdonē (hēdus)* derives from a Greek word that could best be translated as 'pleasure' in English, although the word 'hedonism' is the most obvious rendering. The search for sensual pleasure was a common theme in classic Greek thought.

In the New Testament, the word occurs five times as a noun and five times as a verb. The pleasures of life choke the seed of the Word in the parable of the sower (Luke 8:14). Prayer is not answered because money is spent on pleasures (James 4:1, 3). Carousing in broad daylight is a mistaken idea of pleasure (2 Peter 2:13). While the noun (*hēdonē*) had both good and bad connotations in classical Greek, in the New Testament, it was used only negatively.

Secondly, inward joy (*charein, chara*), the most common New Testament word for joy, occurs 141 times. Perhaps the most notable place is in Philippians, where the obligation to suffer for the gospel's sake is matched by the moral imperative to rejoice in the Lord (Philippians 4:4). Paul is joyful in prayer for the Christians in Philippi (1:24–25), joyful over their generosity (4:10), and can even speak of them as 'his joy and crown' (4:1). He rejoices that even despite false motives, Christ is proclaimed (1:18). The command to rejoice (4:4) is:

> . . . to be sustained by the lofty sense of Christ's redemption, dispelling all anxiety and resolving into trust in God, and with its peace constituting the sure protection for the heart and mind.[9]

In Philippians, it becomes clear that joy is possible even when physical, emotional or spiritual circumstances would seem to mitigate against it. But the overriding focus of joy in the New Testament is the future, for example:

> To him who is able to keep you from stumbling and to present you before his glorious presence without fault and with great joy – to the only God our Saviour be glory, majesty, power and authority, through Jesus Christ our Lord, before all ages, now and for evermore! Amen.
>
> (Jude 24–25)

The suffering and pain of this world are worth enduring for the sake of future joy. This was Jesus' great example of joy for us. On the night before his death, with the certainty of the cross ahead for him and desertion and ultimately persecution for his followers, Jesus told the disciples that their joy could be complete if they kept in obedience to his love (John 15:11).

The Hebrew Christians are encouraged to endure to the point of shedding blood, for Jesus endured even the agony of the cross for the sake of future joy in heaven (Hebrews 12:2). Similarly, the reward of heaven should be enough to enable us to rejoice and 'be happy' when we are insulted, persecuted and falsely accused for Jesus' sake (see Matthew 5:12). This joy comes from being marked out as completely identified with Jesus' priorities and plans, and, with it, the assurance that we will go the way that he has gone.

We sing for joy. We endure hard circumstances because there is joy ahead. And we are commanded to have joy.

Joy, in a nutshell

Clearly, the subject of joy is a big Bible theme. We may summarize the main occurrences of the word as follows:

- Joy comes from an appreciation that the believer is accepted in Christ and loved. Indeed, we should be awestruck by the amazing love and grace that have been lavished on us by the Father in sending the Son (Romans 8:32, 38–39). (More on this in the following chapters.)
- Joy comes from a habitual response to God. The fruit of the Spirit is produced as our sinful nature is crucified and we are led by the Spirit. In other words, the link between a serious attitude toward sin and a life of joy is inextricable. Because sin is our fundamental problem, it is only by first saying 'no' that we can say 'yes'. Christian qualities are not the result of self-improvement. Rather, they are the overflow of a life of abiding in Christ, remaining in him, a life starving the flesh – crucifying it – a life walking in and by the Holy Spirit (see Galatians 5:16–26).
- It has been well said that happiness comes and goes according to our circumstances, but joy comes from the knowledge of our relationship with the Lord. Consequently, even when imprisoned and possibly near martyrdom, Paul can instruct believers to rejoice in the Lord always (hence Philippians 4:11–12). Our joy is found in knowing the truth of Romans 8:28, that is, where Paul states that in all things, God works together for the good of those who love him and are called according to his purpose.[10] God does not make us happy by removing our difficult circumstances; rather, we may find joy through knowing that he is using them to mould us into the image of Jesus.
- Joy is largely future, but is anticipated in the present. It was Jesus' anticipation of heaven's joy that motivated him through the terrible torture of the cross (Hebrews

12:2). It was expected that with the arrival of Jesus on earth, the disciples would be filled with the joy of knowing him and that joy would be complete (John 3:29; 15:11; 16:22–24; 2 John 12). One day, Jesus will return and then God will wipe away every tear (Revelation 7:17; 21:4). On that day, we will be presented without fault and with great joy in the presence of God (Jude 24).

- Joy comes from realizing that we are saved for an eternity with God, in whom is fullness of joy forever. The greatest joy is produced by comprehending the power of the gospel (Matthew 13:20; Luke 2:10; 10:17).

We're now going to look at what two well-known Christian leaders have said about joy.

Christian hedonism

The American pastor and author, John Piper, has the following as his life mission statement, adopted by Bethlehem Baptist Church, Minneapolis: 'God is most glorified in us when we are most satisfied in Him.' With echoes of his hero, Jonathan Edwards, Piper pleads for a pervasive God-centredness in all of life and worship. He contends that our satisfaction, pleasure and delight are not ultimately at odds with God's design for us. God wants us not only to be holy, but also to be happy.

His provocative statement of Christian hedonism modifies the answer to question one of the Westminster Shorter Catechism to: 'Man's chief end is to glorify God *by* enjoying him forever.' By inserting 'by' instead of 'and' in the answer, he argues that our enjoyment of God is not an added extra for the ultra-emotional or enthusiastic Christian, but rather an indication of whether or not God really is our chief end.[11]

For example, if I come home with a dozen red roses, my wife may swing open the front door, see the flowers, fling her arms around me and say, 'Darling, thank you so much. They are wonderful, you shouldn't have bothered.' Would I as a husband respond, 'Well, that's the kind of thing a husband should do, so it's my duty'? No, because a response like that would defeat the purpose and would be considered crass. But if I respond as a loving husband, 'My darling, I love you and I can think of nothing I want more than to do this. It is my pleasure to give you flowers', she is not going to turn to me and say, 'You egotist; it isn't about you!' Rather, my delight in giving flowers dignifies the act, and such pleasure-seeking devotion is a greater indication of love than mere fulfilment of duty.

Thus, Piper argues, the reasoning behind his belief that our *duty* as a Christian is to maximize our *joy* in God.[12]

The joy road

Dr Packer makes the point that the Christian life is not a 'joy ride' but a 'joy road'. To stay on track, we need to change our outlook on life. And, as ever, Jesus is our model for this.

On the night before he dies a painful and cruel death, we find Jesus aligning his will to God's purposes in prayer in the garden of Gethsemane (see Mark 14:32–36). Because of the joy ahead of him, Jesus would endure the agony of the cross (Hebrews 12:3).

So, we should foster the way of joy as a lifestyle, not least by 'fixing our eyes on Jesus, the author and perfecter of faith' (Hebrews 12:2).

Letting joy permeate

Naturally, reviving joy will help dissipate the harmful effects of stress.

Remember that joy will be yours when:

- you know you are accepted by God
- you trust God implicitly
- you conform to God's bigger purposes
- you form good Christian habits
- you realize that heaven is worth the wait.

Joy will be yours in its fullness in heaven!

 Getting personal

Thomas could do with a regular reminder that joy is to be found in living life in harmony with our Creator God. Like many frustrated perfectionists, his outlook on life has become rather cynical, but God has provided other believers to help Thomas keep life's trials in perspective. He would do well to remember the good things God has given him and to pause to give thanks. His sharp mind will give him insights and perspectives that might be missed by other, less observant individuals. But a sense of gratitude and pleasure in all that God has given should help keep Thomas from cynicism.

Stress levels are high in **Anna** and John's household. It is unlikely that their lives will be any less busy in the near future – the time demands from their young twins won't go away soon. It will help Anna if she can seek joy in the little things of life and not have them hurtle by unnoticed. Actively being aware of Jesus in her day-to-day life would be a great goal for her.

What practical suggestions do you have for Anna as she aims to achieve this goal?

10. Relax, you are pre-approved

Long after I was supposed to be tucked up in bed, as a nine-year-old, I can remember sneaking out into the hallway, just around the corner from the living room door. It felt quite daring to listen to grown-up conversations as my parents settled down for a quiet evening without the children.

Here was the opportunity for them to unwind in front of the television and revisit the concerns and issues of the day. And there I was hanging around waiting to hear what they would have to say about me! But inevitably, whenever I came up in conversation, it was with words of disappointment. My parents were usually speaking about their frustrations and concerns about bringing up their children.

Listening into another's conversation rarely brings commendation. Quite often, unguarded remarks out of earshot of the subject is the opportunity to speak plainly about disappointments and concerns.

Feeling slightly guilty

That slightly guilty feeling that I often felt when skulking around the dimly lit hallway after bedtime occasionally returns at coffee time in the church lobby. My mind races ahead of itself: 'That group of three or four people sitting in a huddle deep in conversation must be plotting something without me . . . Should I go near and see whether I can hear something? Should I go over and fish for a compliment or two?'

Paranoia? Maybe. But am I alone in these feelings? I think not. It is my suspicion that many people go through church and family life feeling as though they don't quite make the mark. They feel that people have a condemnatory attitude towards them. Sometimes those feelings are not unjustified. Even our most straightforward communications can have a barb to them. It is possible for a husband to say to his wife, 'Shall I put the children to bed?' with such an inflection, which only the couple would be aware of, that would lead the wife to conclude, 'You mean, "Do I have to do it *again*, even though I only did it last night?"' But, again, often those feelings are little more than paranoia. Learning to appreciate that you are likely to be the only person who is mostly thinking about you is actually rather liberating!

Nevertheless, many people do go through life feeling condemned. Just beneath the surface lurks a desire for approval. Parents feel guilty when they overwork, when they fail to give their children sufficient attention or when their children mess up their lives. Children feel guilty when they fail to live up to their parents' expectations or when their elderly parents hope for more time than the children are real-istically able to give them. The list of stress-inducers is endless. Either I spend my life seeking the approval of others and am hugely deflated when they seem to withhold acceptance, or I live life weighed down by guilt, consistently feeling unworthy. These feelings obviously impact on my stress levels.

This chapter and the following two will delve into slightly deeper theology than we have so far encountered. Sit tight, because the truths and lessons here are foundational. They will reassure you and give you rich resources to draw from during times of difficulty and doubt.

In Christ, you are no longer condemned

A pilot interrupted the flight with an urgent announcement. It was obvious that something was wrong: the plane had passed through some very stormy weather. The crew were racing up and down the aisles, and a passenger had looked out of the window and seen smoke coming from one of the wings. Eventually, in order to allay the passengers' fears, the pilot announced, 'I don't want to alarm you, but I have bad news and good news. The bad news is that the left engine is on fire, some very strong cross-winds have blown us off course, we are completely lost, and it looks like we might need to land in the sea. But the good news is we are making very good time!'

When I first heard that story, it made me think about the fact that many people live life like that. Their final destination is somewhat unknown, but they are going to get there ahead of schedule. No wonder they experience stress.

Romans 8 is wonderfully liberating. If you are 'in Christ Jesus', you are no longer under condemnation. Your guilt has been fully dealt with by Jesus' death on the cross. You have experienced a change of status. When Christ's death is applied to a guilty sinner, he or she passes from condemnation to acceptance and a new status before God. They are now heirs of all the promises made in Christ. Secondly, as a result of this, changes will follow in the area of thinking and feeling. In other words, a changed status leads to a changed state: a new state of mind, a clear conscience, forgiveness and new life. The objective work of 'justification' leads to the subjective witness of assurance.

The key issue addressed in Romans is the fear of death. Many non-Christians will reason, 'If there is no final destination, or if that final destination, for all practical purposes, is unknown, what is the point of trying to seek the approval of God or others?' If a non-believer faces death with no assurance of sins forgiven, then there is some bad news that he or she needs to hear first: without Christ he or she faces condemnation.

But the more subtle issue for Christians in Rome concerned how they lived life every day. They had been justified (their legal status before God had been made right by Christ) and they could face the day of Judgment with the certainty that they would be acquitted and found to be righteous before the law.

The heart of the matter

The anxiety of these Christians in Rome was not so much over their final destination as whether God really had done in them all that he had promised he would do. They probably expected Christ to return in their lifetime. Some had become ill; some had been persecuted – and there was more perse-cution on the horizon – and some were dying. This led them to ask a lot of questions: Am I really forgiven? Can I be sure that I will spend eternity with God? Is my guilt really taken away? Am I a heaven-bound new creation in Christ? And if so, why is it all such hard going?

Romans 8 addresses issues that have to do with the state of the Christian's heart. I have come to see that the doubts to which Paul is responding concern not just the objective state of the Christian's status. They also have much to do with the subjective state of the believer. This, it seems to me, has very direct relevance for us living the Christian life in today's world.

Striving for approval

As C. S. Lewis once observed, the main problem with pride is that it is competitive.[1] My pride is always in competition with someone else's, and I think that I may raise my standing before others by deflating their pride.

A highly competitive person I know once exclaimed, 'We won!' when he heard that his wife was pregnant with their fourth child. His other siblings only had a maximum of three per household.

Others seek approval through their annual appraisal at work, the bonuses they earn at the end of the financial year, the accolades they receive when they score a goal for their team, or in the satisfaction they get when their children obtain coveted places at university.

Seeking the approval of parents, partners, colleagues or friends can be a terrible tyranny, especially when we begin to appreciate that this can be fickle, temporary and based upon performance.

Winston Churchill is well remembered among other things for his famous put-downs. While we may cringe at these condemnatory remarks, we can't help admiring someone who seemed so self-confident.

During the Second World War, he attended a fancy party. Guests could overhear him being upbraided and chided for his arrogance and chauvinism by a very prim and proper-looking lady. She reached the end of her tirade, concluding her chastisement by looking him in the eye and saying, 'Sir, if

I were your wife, I would put poison in your tea.' Winston Churchill, never short of a reply, looked her straight in the eye and said, 'Lady, if you were my wife, I would drink it.'

In his biography on Winston Churchill, Roy Jenkins records many items of Churchill's confident and exhaustive correspondence to Prime Minister Asquith in 1912–14, and to David Lloyd George later that decade. But despite his hawkish stance and his brilliant leadership during the Second World War, Winston Churchill was not as thick-skinned as he often appeared.[2] Churchill spent many years battling what he called his 'black dog of depression'. It was only as he threw himself into the business of overcoming the tyranny of Hitler's army that he put to the back of his mind all of the self-esteem and confidence issues with which he had wrestled.

Of course, this was not really a cure. In the modern age, we are much more aware that professional help is often required to deal with depression. Moreover, while being undoubtedly an outstanding leader, Winston Churchill might not necessarily be the best example of how a Christian should apply ancient Christian truths to life today. Nevertheless, this example shows that every one of us can wrestle with self-doubt and lack of personal assurance from time to time. At different stages of our lives, we may be more acutely aware of issues of self-worth than at other times. Being a parent will definitely bring things to the fore. So too will occasions when our career does not go according to plan, or we wrestle with poor health, or we face the challenges of old age.

Romans 8 is here to help us apply the gospel message into our deepest heart needs. The gospel is intended to impact on how we feel and how we should respond to God with every part of our being.

Paul wants Christians to have confidence in the character of God himself. Promises of joy, freedom from worry, and godly ambition, for example, are groundless if they are not based in the truths found in Romans 8. This is not a message of escapism. Rather, contentment is found in truly knowing the liberating message of 'no condemnation'.

No condemnation? Really?

Romans 8:1–3

Therefore, there is now no condemnation for those who are in Christ Jesus, because through Christ Jesus the law of the Spirit who gives life has set you free from the law of sin and death. For what the law was powerless to do because it was weakened by the flesh, God did by sending his own Son in the likeness of sinful flesh to be a sin offering. And so he condemned sin in the flesh.

It's worth reminding ourselves of some foundational truths.

Christians are freed from condemnation because they are 'in Christ Jesus'. In other words, they are 'declared right' and 'justified'. Christ's death has set us free from the wrath and judgment of God. It's liberating!

This great act of liberation happened 2,000 years ago. While we were still powerless to justify ourselves, God did it for us by sending his Son to be a sin offering. But experientially and personally, this liberation happened to me when Christ's death was worked out in my life (v. 3).

What does it mean for a guilty sinner, like you or me, not to be condemned by the ultimate Judge? He who, above all people, looks beyond appearances and knows the rottenness inside?

Christ was condemned for us

Christ was condemned for us (v. 3). The implications are huge. Christ was a real human being, but, significantly, a sinless human being. Hence, he was able to become a 'sin offering'. Paul emphasizes this point elsewhere: 'God made him who had no sin to be sin for us, so that in him we might become the righteousness of God' (2 Corinthians 5:21). We can enjoy 'no condemnation' because Christ took upon himself the full weight of the judgment of God and thereby was condemned for us.

Christians have found great comfort in these words of Isaiah, which predict the work of Christ on the cross:

> . . . he was pierced for our transgressions,
>   he was crushed for our iniquities;
> the punishment that brought us peace was on him,
>   and by his wounds we are healed.
> We all, like sheep, have gone astray,
>   each of us has turned to his own way;
> and the LORD has laid on him
>   the iniquity of us all.
> (Isaiah 53:5–6)

Romans 8:3–4

For what the law was powerless to do because it was weakened by the flesh, God did by sending his own Son in the likeness of sinful flesh to be a sin offering. And so he condemned sin in the flesh, in order that the righteous requirement of the law might be fully met in us, who do not live according to the flesh but according to the Spirit.

Christ met the law's demands in us

It is worth considering the impact of what Paul goes on to say: not only was Christ condemned for us, but the demands of the law have now been met in us.

Paul has already been quite blunt: the full demands of the law cannot be met *by* us, 'for all have sinned and fall short of the glory of God' (Romans 3:23). But God has a plan both to uphold the exacting standards of the law and, at the same time, acquit the guilty.

Christ met the demands of the law *for* us. He paid the legal penalty for our sin by dying the death of a condemned man (see Romans 6:23). God accepted this full payment of our debt and in return gives a free, undeserved gift to us sinful human beings.

God declares that because of what Jesus has done, guilty sinners may now be in a right standing in the eyes of the law. When God opens the law book to bring me to justice on the last day, before me there will be a list of all my trespasses and iniquities and sin. And, in a sense, rubber-stamped next to that list will be the words: 'no condemnation', because Christ became sin for me.

A sixteenth-century German monk called Martin Luther believed that the Catholic Church had lost its way on this great gospel truth. Salvation could not be bought. Acceptance with God was a gift that he alone could give on the basis of Jesus' saving death. This truth gripped him, and the gospel rippled out across the whole of Europe. He wrote this:

> Our most merciful Father sent His only Son into the world and laid upon him the sins of all men saying: be thou Peter that denier, Paul that persecutor, blasphemer and cruel oppressor, David that adulterer, that sinner that did eat the fruit in paradise, that thief that hanged upon the cross, and

be thou the person which hath committed the sins of all. See therefore that thou pay and satisfy for them.[3]

Christian truth needs to be 'worked in' and 'worked out'

It seems to me that twenty-first-century Christians need to recall, and keep calling to mind, this great truth: Christ was condemned for me; the law's demands have been met in me.

Is this not liberating?

Somebody once said, 'The nice thing about being imperfect is the joy you know it gives to other people.' There is a certain ring of truth to this! We can be rather good at inflicting guilt upon one another within our Christian communities. We have performance expectations and exert pressure for people to conform to many things that have more to do with the culture of our community than gospel standards. The church is supposed to be a place of acceptance and free grace. But it is often, by contrast, the place where guilt is induced.

Martin Luther found the gospel to be so liberating. He had found the unreformed church to be a place of condemnation and guilt, until he met Jesus. He wrote of that marvellous experience in the preface to his commentary on Galatians quoted above:

When I understood [the imputation of Christ's righteousness], and when the concept of justification by faith alone burst through into my mind, suddenly it was like the doors of paradise swung open and I walked through.[4]

I believe that when we grasp the full significance of these gospel truths, like Luther, we too will feel a tremendous sense of liberation.

Approval and stress

Here are some questions to consider:

- **Does knowing God's approval motivate me to be ambitious?** (Refer also to chapter 7.) This is sometimes succinctly described as working 'from grace', not 'for grace'. Because I am forgiven and accepted, I can be a risk-taker, for my status is not tied up with my own success. I can be bold (because the gospel message is true), and I can be generous with time and money (because God has already outgiven me).
- **Have I inculcated the habit of tracing feelings of guilt back to their source?** We have noted that guilty feelings are very debilitating and can make a person very stressed. Before dealing with the symptoms (guilty feelings), it is first necessary to see whether the primary cause has been dealt with (guilt). A friend of mine had to have a toe cut off because it was so badly infected that it could not be saved. However, she continued to feel excruciating pain in that part of her foot even though the toe no longer existed. False guilt can be like that. The radical surgery has been done, but phantom pain can still be felt.
- **Do I spend too much of my time trying to earn the approval of my boss, my spouse or my parents?** We are certainly encouraged by the Bible to be responsible towards our boss, spouse and parents.[5] However, the desire to please should be motivated by love, not by some false sense that I will gain my worth as a human being by seeking to be perfect. Moreover, having an unrealistic expectation of perfection in this life will undoubtedly induce guilt and increase stress. We could

well be more loving towards others in our family, work
and social circles by first ensuring that we are secure in
God's love and assured of the acquittal from guilt that
Christ has achieved on the cross for us.

Sometimes, it might be helpful to have a mature
Christian friend, or even a counsellor, to assist us in
answering these questions:

- *Should I feel guilty?* If so, apologize to God and the
  offended party.
- *Is the guilt false?* If so, bring it to mind and ask God
  to cleanse your thinking.
- *Have I really experienced and felt God's forgiveness and
  acceptance?* Enjoy the liberty that all of this brings!

 Getting personal

Today's working mothers are particularly stretched and
often feel overburdened by the need to 'juggle' without
dropping too many balls. To both **Susan** and **Anna**, I
would like to say: 'Bring your guilt and guilty feelings to
God and refresh yourself in the knowledge that Christ
was condemned in order that you need not be. You are
pre-approved!' How liberating is that?

Read this chapter slowly and prayerfully, noting verses
and thoughts that will strengthen your faith and enable
you to encourage others.

11. Let God be King

William Ernest Henley's *Invictus* is a popular choice of reading at modern funerals. However, the Christian will realize that the best answer to stress is to bring to mind that: '*God* is the master of my fate; *he* is the captain of my soul. I am not.'[1]

Despite marvellous medical advances, Psalm 90:10 is generally still true: 'The days of our years are threescore years and ten; and if by reason of strength they be fourscore years, yet is their strength labour and sorrow; for it is soon cut off, and we fly away' (KJV).

Some lessons take a lifetime to learn. My pneumonia incident was part of an ongoing work of God in my life, I believe, designed to remind me that I am not in control. The quicker I get off the throne and allow the sovereign God to reign, the quicker stress will start to play a less dominant part of my life.

I can also think of a couple of other illnesses from which I should have learned this lesson. In my late teens, I experienced bad migraines. Lying down in a darkened room helped a bit.

I was in the middle of exams and, with hindsight, the stress of those exams was certainly likely to have contributed. I met up with a friend to pray, quite long prayers well into the night. Mysteriously, things seemed to get worse. Looking back, I think I would now conclude: shorter prayer times, less intense cramming, and some rest and sleep would have done me more good and would have been pleasing to God. Moreover, this might also have reduced the migraines.

A few years later, I contracted a post-viral ailment that made me exhausted, burnt out, and eventually caused me to be off work for several months. But again with the clarity of hindsight, I can see that long working days followed by evenings studying for banking qualifications and then weekends overcommitted in the life of the church were the main contributory factors. Less self-induced stress and more rest would have been better.

We have seen that there is an inbuilt rhythm of work and rest that God has ordained in the created world. I eventually learned that lesson. But decades later, I think I can also look back and *thank* God for reminders of my own mortality, reminders that I am ultimately not in control, reminders that he used even migraines, post-viral illness and pneumonia for my good. Through these things, he taught me empathy, helped me conform to the likeness of Christ, assisted me to be less driven and less full of my own self-importance, and, ultimately, enabled me to prepare for my heavenly home.

Romans 8:28

And we know that in all things God works for the good of those who love him, who have been called according to his purpose.

As we observed previously, Romans 8:28 focuses our attention on all the things (like death, life, illness and a sense of our mortality) that God uses to make us more like Christ.

However, we would be very odd people indeed if we never wrestled with the tension: 'How on earth is God working out his purposes in this or that particular circumstance?'

Non-Christian, and Christian, answers to the problem of evil

Buddhism teaches that suffering is not real, but an illusion. According to this teaching, suffering is related to our yet-unfulfilled desire for things. For example, if I'm hungry, I suffer because I desire food. Once the desire is satiated, I no longer suffer. Or if I'm ill, my perception of suffering stems from my desire for health, rather than from the illness itself. Similarly, evil in this world should be shunned, and temptation resisted. If I do away with the desire by adopting the path of Buddhism, then I will no longer suffer.

The basic teaching of Hinduism is that people suffer because they deserve it. Hinduism (unlike Buddhism) teaches that suffering is very real. If there appears to be no reason for a particular instance of suffering, then it's because of something we've done in a previous life.

Muslims believe that all suffering is determined by Allah, who cannot ever suffer, but rather is the cause all suffering. God is the 'unmoved Mover'; he is impassive to suffering, so the only response is to submit to the will of Allah. Questioning the suffering would be blasphemous.

The atheist answer to suffering at best seems to be as follows: God cannot exist because there is suffering in the world. 'If God is all-loving and all-powerful, then why is there suffering?' Suffering is meaningless. It is the random by-product of a universe driven by chance. There's no reason for it, no design behind it, no comfort in it and no pity, because it's a case of the survival of the fittest, and that's just the way things are. It's all about natural selection.

In the previous section in Romans 8, Paul has outlined a pattern of Christian living which can be encapsulated in the phrase: 'suffering, then glory'. The groaning creation (v. 22), the groaning Christian (v. 23) and the groaning Spirit (v. 26) all prepare us for the future completion of God's plans.

Modern readers struggle to make the connection in Romans 8:28. Here Paul is demonstrating how our weaknesses and God's purposes are inextricably linked together. The Christian life is very paradoxical. Present sufferings are not just a necessary endurance before glory, but rather the very means by which God prepares me for the next life. In our weakness, we find God most actively at work in our heart and circumstances.

This is a very different perspective from that of the world, and, in fact, from most other world views.[2]

Christianity: a unique answer to the problem of stress

Romans 8 is not trying to answer the big questions about suffering in the world. Rather, in this passage, Paul addresses the complex question: 'Why do Christians suffer?'

I have some sympathy with the comment attributed to St Teresa of Avila: 'God, if this is the way you treat your friends, it's no wonder you have so many enemies!' Nevertheless, Romans 8:28 asserts that God is at work for good amidst stresses, pain and difficulties. Moreover, if we gain the outlook on life that Paul encourages, we will begin to view these struggles from a fresh perspective.

I believe that God used physical ailments to remind me of my mortality. He helped me to release control and also to appreciate that I had a part to play in the building of his kingdom here on earth.

Noticing the scope of what Paul writes in this verse is important:

- *In all things*: Everything is included, all life's circumstances. God is not powerless and impotent as the atheist assumes, but sovereign over all.
- *God works*: This is neither fatalism, nor some impersonal force at work, but providential oversight of a good God.
- *For good*: That is, as defined by God and not me, for my holiness and Christlike maturing.
- *For those who love him*: This is a promise made to Christians that God will use life's circumstances for our good – it's not a universal promise to all.
- *According to his purposes*: God fulfils his plans, not least as outlined in Romans 9 – 11.

Practical implications

Here are some very practical implications of Romans 8:28.

Firstly, I absolutely believe Romans 8:28 to be true. However, this verse does not mean that we will always know the reason for what God is doing in our lives. In fact, the verse offers confidence that *God* knows what is good for me, even if I don't always know that for myself. He does not owe me an explanation!

Secondly, Paul's 'thorn in the flesh' (2 Corinthians 12) led him to cry out to God in his weakness. Despite his persistent prayer, he came to realize that God might keep him weak in order that he (God) would get the glory in all things. Being made aware of our frailty is a good thing. God might introduce things into my life that will bring about my humbling.

Thirdly, this verse does not merely counsel us to make the best of our circumstances. Rather, and more positively, it states that God uses even the most difficult circumstances for his greater-good purposes. The specific goal of God's purposes is that we might be conformed to the likeness of Christ. Thus, everything in me that does not look like Jesus, he chisels off.

Fourthly, Christians should remember that God worked all things together to bring us to Christ, and he will continue to work all things together to bring us to glory.

Romans 8:29–30

For those God foreknew he also predestined to be conformed to the image of his Son, that he might be the firstborn among many brothers and sisters. And those he predestined, he also called; those he called, he also justified; those he justified, he also glorified.

Romans 8:29–30 contains two key words: 'foreknow' and 'predestine'. They are words full of rich theology and, once better understood, I believe they should bring comfort to stressed people.

Comforting truths

1. God loves you unconditionally

'Foreknow' means 'to know in advance'
Sometimes people have taken 'foreknow' to mean that God knew in advance who would respond to the gospel. In other

words, because he foreknew, God then set their destinies. It seems to me that this shaves off the uncomfortable idea that God has actually predestined us since before the foundation of the world as to who will or who will not become Christians.[3] But a careful reading of the text should not lead to this conclusion.

However, we will learn to welcome this teaching when we appreciate that 'foreknowledge' is a relational word. To 'know' in the Bible is not so much knowing about something, but rather having a relationship with somebody. In fact, 'know' is almost synonymous with the idea of love. Some translations have written this verse as 'those God fore-loved'. To 'know' implies great intimacy and knowledge. Israel, as God's chosen people, knew this to be true:

> The LORD did not set his affection on you and choose you
> because you were more numerous than other peoples, for you
> were the fewest of all peoples. But it was because the LORD
> loved you and kept the oath he swore to your ancestors that
> he brought you out with a mighty hand and redeemed you
> from the land of slavery.
> (Deuteronomy 7:7–8)

True love requires no other reason to be loving

Suppose I say to my wife, Carrie, 'My darling, why, out of all the men whom you could have married, did you decide to marry me?' If she responds, 'Well Simon, out of all the men that I have known, you were really the most useful for my purposes', this would not be the most flattering of statements!

However, if she responds, 'Simon, I love you and I want to spend the rest of my married life with you for no other reason than I love you', that makes sense; the choice is for no other reason than that she loves me. 'Well, why do you love me?' 'I love you because I love you.' It's a self-answering question. This is also the only reason that God gives to justify his choice. It has nothing to do with my merit, but rests purely on his choosing love. It was through love that he predestined us (see Ephesians 1:4–5).

2. God is in absolute control

'Predestine' means 'to determine in advance'

What does it mean to say that those whom God foreknew, he predestined?

J. I. Packer responds to the question: if God chooses in advance, why should we then bother doing evangelism?

> Two facts show this: in the first place you give thanks for your conversion – now why would you do that? Well, because you know in your heart that God was entirely responsible for it. You did not save yourself, he saved you. There is a second way in which you acknowledge that God is sovereign in salvation, you pray for the conversion of others. You ask God to work in them everything necessary for their salvation. On our feet we may have arguments about it but on our knees we are all agreed.[4]

Even those who seem to deny the sovereignty of God in salvation show by their actions that they do believe him to be sovereign.

So what is comforting and assuring about the doctrine of predestination? Exactly this: God is King!

Six great encouragements about the Romans 8 view of predestination

1. It gives me confidence that some people will be saved

Ephesians 2 accentuates the fact that we are spiritually dead outside of Christ. John 9 emphasizes that we are blind until Christ opens our eyes. Romans 5 states that we are weak and powerless outside of his love.

Heaven will be filled with a crowd that no-one can number (Revelation 7:9 – think how huge that must be). But we could have no confidence that anyone would be in heaven without God's sovereign choice. He hasn't left it to chance or human will, but to sovereign preordination.

2. It gives God his rightful credit: salvation is his work

Paul says, 'Those he predestined, he also called; those he called, he also justified; those he justified, he also glorified' (Romans 8:30). This is God's work. Nothing glorifies God more than saving sinful people. He does what we can't do for ourselves. Amidst the pain over God's chosen people, Israel, rejecting the message about Jesus, Paul concludes with 11:33–36, rejoicing in God's inscrutable and eternally wise plans.

The point of this doctrine is to bring comfort to believers that God will never let us down and never give us up. Hence the stunning conclusion in Romans 11:33–36:

> Oh, the depth of the riches of the wisdom and knowledge
> of God!
> How unsearchable his judgments,
> and his paths beyond tracing out!
> 'Who has known the mind of the Lord?
> Or who has been his counsellor?'

'Who has ever given to God,
   that God should repay them?'
For from him and through him and for him are all things.
   To him be the glory forever! Amen.

To paraphrase the immortal words of Magnus Magnusson, God has started, so he will finish. God, who began a good work in us, will bring it to completion. If God did not predestine, then I would have to be in control of everything in my life. How stressful would that be?

Sometimes, life will seem perplexing, or our suffering will appear overwhelming, or our plans seem to come to nothing. At such times, it is good to remember that we will be groaning until glory, but we are not alone: the Spirit groans alongside us (see Romans 8:22–27).

Can you bring yourself to pray: 'God, make me weak, so that you may get glory for yourself'? Paul learned to boast in his weakness, and he found that God's power is perfected in weakness. This sounds disempowering, but ironically, it is one of the greatest releases from stress that I know.

God gives us what we need, not necessarily what we ask for

If Romans 8:28 is true, then at the very least it will free me from fear of what the future holds (hence vv. 38–39). This little poem puts it so well:

I asked God for strength, that I might achieve.
   I was made weak, that I might learn humbly to obey.
I asked for health, that I might do greater things.
   I was given infirmity, that I might do better things.
I asked for riches, that I might be happy.
   I was given poverty, that I might be wise.

I asked for power, that I might have the praise of men.

I was given weakness, that I might feel the need of God.

I asked for all things, that I might enjoy life.

I was given life that I might enjoy all things.

I got nothing that I asked for – but everything I had hoped for.

Almost despite myself, my unspoken prayers were
answered.

I am, among all men, most richly blessed.

(Anon)[5]

3. It gives me assurance

When I trained to be a Red Cross lifeguard, we were taught the lifesaving grip. The rescuer grabs the forearm of the person needing rescuing. They in turn grab your forearm. The double lock gives extra security. But it is still quite clear who is doing the saving and which grip really counts.

The ground of my assurance is not my grasp of God. My grip is weak and unable to stay clinging to his arm with my own strength alone. But his grasp of me is strong and secure. This should encourage me to realize that he is not suddenly going to let go of me and drop his grip. He has eternal purposes at stake.

4. It humbles me to realize that he chose me for no other reason than he set his love on me

But, people worry, 'Why did he *not* choose others; surely this is so unfair?'

It was nothing other than God setting his love upon his chosen ones in advance, thus resulting in him determining that they would indeed be saved.

Perhaps this illustration will help: I think of good friends of ours who have adopted several children from very tricky backgrounds with a variety of physical, mental and social challenges, providing them with a loving Christian home. We marvel at their love and sacrifice. I have not yet heard anyone say to them, 'How heartless of you not to adopt *all* needy children.' Rather, people are astounded at their selfless grace.

It is good to remember that it is the love of God that determines whether anyone will be in heaven. After all, imagine what heaven would be like if it was dependent on human merit and choice. Actually, it wouldn't be heaven at all. It would be full of prudish, proud pigs!

5. It drives me to prayer

As I pray for my non-believing friends and relations, the doctrine of predestination makes me very conscious that if God doesn't open blind eyes and raise spiritually dead people, then however much I may try to explain it all to them, they will remain spiritually lost. Having friends and family who are spiritually lost could well be a cause of stress, but the best possible response is to pray for them.

John Newton's hymn, *Amazing Grace*, captures this sentiment in the line: ''Twas grace that taught my heart to fear *and* grace my fears relieved.'

Jesus told three poignant parables about being lost, involving a sheep, a coin and a son (see Luke 15). Lost sheep cry out, but the shepherd seeks and saves them. God is committed to seeking and saving the lost, and he invites us to participate in this mission, in part through prayer.

6. It encourages me to endure, because the work of predestination is not finished until my glorification

If God has set his love upon me, then I will play my part in responding to grace until I come to glory and the process is finished.

His love for me is greater and more powerful than my love for him. But my love for him flows from his marvellous prior love (my grasp of him).

How does all this help with stress?

We may be confident that God will do his work. And, because we have this confidence, we may also do our work.

I believe in a sovereign God. He is in control. Hallelujah! OK, so I may not always welcome the difficult circumstances that come my way. Think about Joseph: he endured terrible treatment at the hands of his brothers, resulting in him being sold into slavery. But am I able to look at my suffering and say along with Joseph, 'You [or my circumstances] intended to harm me, but God intended it for good' (Genesis 50:20)?

God is in control of his world. Is that not a great stress-relief?

Attitudes

My thinking needs to be aligned to God's plans for all things – to bring them to unity under Christ the head (see Ephesians 1). This must change my attitude and outlook on life.

The following blog post expressed it far better than I can. Ruth van den Broek writes about her conscious effort to maintain a healthy Christian attitude towards her suffering:

> My attitude to Cystic Fibrosis has changed a great deal over the past few years. I used to think of it as an evil, external thing. I need to be able to see it as a result of the fall. But I also need to see it as a gift that was chosen for me before time began and was given to me by the Father who knows how to give good gifts to his children.
>
> I need to see it as one of the main shapers of my life.

I need to see who I might have been without it.

I need to see how it has helped to change David [her husband] for the better.

I need to see the eternal perspective it has helped us live with.

I need to see the people we've been able to meet and chat to because of it.

I need to see the lessons in patience and trust and many, many other things.

I need to see how many times Cystic Fibrosis has forced us to our knees in prayer.

I need to be able to thank God for [my illness] and mean it.

I think it is so important that I don't see Cystic Fibrosis as this thing that my doctors and I are fighting. That image takes away all of the good things. It changes me from a suffering person, helpless and needy before my God, to a person who, empowered by modern medicine and my own strength, can make it through illness. I pray that I would get better, but my job is absolutely not to spend my life fighting to keep my earthly body alive as long as possible.

Of course, my body is important. But the longer I live, the more I am convinced that an aggressive attitude to our illnesses and diseases is not a faithful one. When I am aggressive towards the tool in the hand of the Master Craftsman, then I miss His ultimate vision, I forget the necessity of every blow and I also fail to see the kindness in His eyes.

If I see Cystic Fibrosis as an enemy, that attitude is not only likely to stifle my thankfulness but also to turn me away from the gospel path of rejoicing in weakness. I want to spend my life learning ever more that strength truly is found in weakness and that, thanks to God and His use of Cystic Fibrosis, I get stronger every day in the ways that really matter.[6]

Awe, worship and contentment

Why, out of all the people on the earth, did God choose to save me? Because he set his love on me. What a marvel! My short-sightedness and self-centredness will slowly dissipate when I ponder the great goodness of God and his divine condescension in rescuing even me.

If I can carve out space in a busy week to take in the sovereign purposes of God, then this will be time well spent. Among other things, this should bring a true sense of contentment in my life. Paul speaks in terms of learning this secret. It's an open secret that really should be shared with all stressed people.

> I am not saying this because I am in need, for I have learned to be content whatever the circumstances . . .

> . . . Godliness with contentment is great gain.
> (Philippians 4:11; 1 Timothy 6:6)

 Getting personal

Is **Thomas** happy with his lot in life? Clearly not. He will need to keep checking his natural attitudes towards things. He finds it all too easy to be cynical. And because he sets himself high standards, he does not suffer fools gladly. He is restless and rarely content.

Spending some time consciously and proactively recognizing God's goodness and thanking him for his many blessings will help Thomas. Even though it may take time for the reality to sink in, I believe that meditating on Romans 8 will be cathartic for him. I believe that if Thomas allows the rich truths of Romans 8 to sink in, he will marvel afresh at God's sovereign, providential purposes. This should make him truly grateful and content.

Jack would do well to remember that God is still working out his purposes, which will not be completed until he has perfected us. This encourages our active cooperation with the Holy Spirit and a determination to live in line with God's good plans for our life. Confidence in God's work is not intended to bring passivity, but rather to motivate us to work for his glory.

To **Susan** and **Anna** I would say, 'Find contentment in who God is: he is for you; he is working in the complexities and mundaneness of your demanding lives to conform you to Christ's likeness. He is actively at work in your circumstances. Pray that he will open your eyes so that you can see this!'

Do you know any 'Susans' or 'Annas' whom you can encourage with the words of this chapter?

12. Remember that God is for you!

A well-known Christian leader gave me a lift back from a meeting in his car. I was interested that the CD he was playing was the soundtrack to *Bridget Jones's Diary*. 'I love this film,' he commented. I was a little surprised. The morality of the film and the world view it espouses can hardly be in sync with a Christian outlook, even though parts of it are very funny.

However, when I voiced my thoughts, his response was very interesting. He said, 'You need to see past most of the movie and understand what it is that people are really looking for. The world is crying out for love. The Bridget Joneses of this world look for love in a romantic escapism. But the gospel offers them what they are really looking for, even if they do not yet know it.'

Playing at sex but looking for love

This is very true. The world is looking for love. This can be seen in many ways:

- Despite the cynical expectation that true love is hard to find and unlikely to last forever, Hollywood movie-makers know that the romantic 'boy meets girl/girl meets boy and (eventually) they live happily ever after' genre makes big bucks.

Or:

- Look at people's Facebook statuses. Alongside pictures of meals with friends, funny one-liners they have heard or pictures of their families, within the space of a dozen or so words, many of our statuses reveal our desire for affection from our virtual friends. Perhaps this is best encapsulated in the following widely used Facebook status: 'I just want to find someone who will love me for exactly who I am pretending to be.'

However, attempting to find unconditional and lasting love in the wrong places will fuel stress. Such stress may come in the form of an unrealistic idealism. ('I want to be perfect/live in a perfect world.') It may come in the form of constantly seeking affirmation and approval. ('I need to prove to you that I am great/the best at everything.') Or it may emerge in the form of feelings of insecurity and unworthiness. ('I need to be loved and don't know where to find love.')

G. K. Chesterton put it succinctly and well: 'Every man who knocks on the door of a brothel is looking for God.'[1]

Paul concludes Romans 8 with words intended to focus our minds and hearts on God's wonderful character. Being accepted and loved in Christ brings confidence and assurance that will be found nowhere else. Our striving for perfection is satisfied in knowing a good and perfect God. Our insecurities and need for approval are met in the gospel message. My desire to feel valued and worth something is satisfied because of the steadfast love of God in Christ Jesus.

It seems to me that truly knowing these Christian principles offers us the most marvellous resources to enable us to live as we were intended to live, amidst the complexities of twenty-first-century expectations and lifestyles.

Rich resources from Romans

Notice four things in particular:

Romans 8:31–34

What, then, shall we say in response to these things? If God is for us, who can be against us? He who did not spare his own Son, but gave him up for us all – how will he not also, along with him, graciously give us all things? Who will bring any charge against those whom God has chosen? It is God who justifies. Who then is the one who condemns? No one. Christ Jesus who died – more than that, who was raised to life – is at the right hand of God and is also interceding for us.

---

1. 'If God is for us, who can be against us?'

When life is tough, it is tempting for the Christian to ask, 'Is God really for me?' There is a plethora of circumstances ranging from global, national or local disasters to personal health, work / financial challenges and relationship difficulties, which might lead an individual to question whether God is actively involved in the circumstances of life.

Paul's answer to: 'Is God for us?' can be found supremely in the fact that God did not even spare his own Son for us. It is Christ:

- who died
- who rose again
- who is at the right hand
- who is interceding.

Paul invites us to look at the equation. If God has given all this, what could possibly stack up against it? God took on the world, the flesh and the devil – and won.

We need regularly to remind ourselves: 'God is for me.' When stress is piling up in my body, and I perhaps feel particularly out of control or unloved or unfocused, I have to remember right then and there: God is for me!

The first half of Paul's letter to the Romans uses legal and forensic language to describe a judicial process that climaxes in the acquittal of guilty sinners. Paul discusses the conundrum of how guilty sinners may apparently be 'let off' by a just judge. He proceeds to explain that it is by the penalty for sin being paid by the Son of God.[2] Thus, the gospel message is not so much, 'God loves me', but rather, 'God loved me' (Galatians 2:20). I am placed in a right relationship with God when I appreciate all that Christ did for me on the cross.

However, here in Romans chapter 8, Paul wants to be sure that we do not miss the key point that the impact of the gospel is felt at a very intimate level. The love of God in Christ Jesus (Romans 8:35, 37, 39) is something I can know: it's personal. God is for you in the way a father is for his son: on the touchlines of the football match, cheering you on – not because you are necessarily the star player, but simply because he is your father and you are his son. He is for you in the way that a father will scoop up his tired toddler and cuddle her in his arms because she is too tired to walk any further by herself.

Let me illustrate this point from another part of the Bible: the apostle John describes God's unveiling of the reality of heaven through a marvellous and terrifying vision (Revelation 1:9–20). Awful though this sight is, the purpose of the apocalypse is in order that his readers may understand: 'To him who loves us and has freed us from our sins by his blood, and has made us to be a kingdom and priests to serve his God and Father – to him be glory and power forever and ever! Amen' (Revelation 1:5–6).

The prayer we should pray when reading Revelation is: 'Lord, open my eyes to the unseen reality of Christ.' The present reality is tough, but through the eyes of faith, we peek behind the curtain and see a victorious Christ surrounded by a huge throng of victorious worshippers. At the heart of the universe is a God of love. This is reality, and one day my present experience will catch up with it.

2. Nothing can separate you

> **Romans 8:35–36**
>
> Who shall separate us from the love of Christ? Shall trouble or hardship or persecution or famine or nakedness or danger or sword? As it is written:
>
> 'For your sake we face death all day long;
>   we are considered as sheep to be slaughtered.'

When we suffer, it feels very personal. We ask, 'Why me? What have I done to deserve this? God, why did you let this happen to me?' And, in a very real sense, when I suffer, it gets to *me*. No-one else can understand the pain I feel. It is very lonely and isolating. As the old spiritual says, 'Nobody knows the trouble I've seen, nobody knows my sorrow . . .'[3]

Perhaps, for this reason, Paul personalizes the perceived threats (v. 31). He does not say, 'What can separate us?', but rather, 'Who can separate us?'.

There are principalities and powers at work behind the onslaughts that we experience. Paul assumes that Christians will experience trouble,[4] hardship, persecution, famine, nakedness, danger or sword. Some of this suffering is common to all, because we live in a fallen world; some comes from direct persecution.

Paul quotes from Psalm 44:22: we are 'like sheep to be slaughtered'. In the psalm, the writer speaks of severe suffering, and yet consistently affirms that he will not falter.

It feels very personal. But Paul states that spiritual abandonment will not separate you, nor will active persecution, nor the suffering of being in this world. None of these will be able to separate us from God. Why not? Because of the love of Christ: he who bore the shame, the pain and the curse on the cross.

Paul's biggest comfort for Christians living in a suffering world is to consider the fact that God sent his Son – and Jesus willingly came to earth in order to go to the cross for the sake of our sins. As Timothy Keller says,

> The only love that won't disappoint you is one that can't change, that can't be lost, that is not based on the ups and downs of life or on how well you live. It is something that not even death can take away from you. God's love is the only thing like that.[5]

How big is your current trial? Have you been convinced that nothing can separate you from God's love?

3. You will be more than conqueror

> **Romans 8:37**
>
> No, in all these things we are more than conquerors through him who loved us.

The comfort of this verse is found at the communal level, rather than just the individual one. 'God loved us,' says Paul. Though the church may at times seem defeated and downtrodden, Paul nevertheless takes comfort in the fact that they will be 'more than conquerors' or 'super victorious'.

The basis of this victory is not primarily dependent on our love and dedication to God. Rather, here, as in the next verse, there is a sense in which we are passive in the process of being victorious. The comfort is to be found in the certainty that God loves us, and this is not based on our feeble and faltering love for him.

In the previous chapter of this book, we noted that our love for God gives us assurance (Romans 8:28). Here, in Romans 8:37, Paul concentrates on God's love for us. It is because of his persistent love that we will persevere.

The basis of our victory is not down to our dedication and commitment to God, although that has to happen in order that we will find God to be true. But the basis is God's own love. The sentiment is well expressed as follows:

> Hate can make a man a conqueror, can fill him with furious energy, but only love can make him more-than-conqueror.[6]

It is the love of God that energizes, motivates and fortifies us. God's commitment to us tempers our drive and ambition. His favourable disposition towards us is both strengthening and liberating. I have nothing to prove. He has proved himself faithful.

What accounts for this great victory that is ours in Christ? The hostile world is able to throw the very worst suffering at us – and Nero's persecution of Christians was certainly awful – but there is hope in our identification with Christ. As Jesus himself said, 'If the world hates you, keep in mind that it hated me first' (John 15:18). Paul does not assume that suffering is a cause for doubting God's love. Christ's conquering love was excruciatingly painful, but when we suffer in Christ and like Christ, we show our true union with him. Hence,

> The true Christian way of living, the true Christian joy
> in living, comes to us not in spite of our tribulation,
> disappointment, or even sin, but because of them . . . we have
> something left over when life and death have done their worst.[7]

The ability to triumph over adversity does not arise because Christians are stronger, or because they have more stable personalities, or because they are wealthier, or because they have some superiority over those around them. The basis of their victory is Christ's victory. Knowing this should be a great relief indeed.

In the early eighteenth century, John Newton contemplated the cross and all that it had achieved for him. In the last verse of the hymn below, he concludes how the impact of pondering on the cross affected his outlook on this life and the next:

> In evil long I took delight
> Un-awed by shame or fear
> Till a new object struck my sight
> And stopped my wild career.

I saw one hanging on a tree
In agonies and blood
He fixed his languid eyes on me
As near his cross I stood.

Sure never till my latest breath
Can I forget that look.
It seemed to charge me with his death
Tho' not a word he spoke.

My conscience owned and felt the guilt
And plunged me in despair.
I saw my sins his blood has spilt
And helped to nail him there.

Alas I knew not what I did
But now my tears are vain.
Where shall my trembling soul be hid
For I the Lord have slain.

A second look he gave which said
Freely all forgive.
This blood is for thy ransom paid
I die that thou mayest live.

Thus while his death my sin displays
In all its blackest hue
Such is the mystery of grace
It seals my pardon too.

With pleasing grief and mournful joy
My spirit now is filled.
That I should such a life destroy
Yet live by him I killed.

4. You can be sure

Romans 8:38–39

For I am convinced that neither death nor life, neither angels nor demons, neither the present nor the future, nor any powers, neither height nor depth, nor anything else in all creation, will be able to separate us from the love of God that is in Christ Jesus our Lord.

In Romans 8:38, Paul can say, 'For I am persuaded . . . I am convinced . . .'

This super-victory begins with a conviction. Paul does not say, 'I have convinced / persuaded myself'; rather, he has been persuaded by the marvellous love of Christ. The gospel has won him over. Every other potential threat to his certainty is overthrown.

- Neither death nor life
- Neither angels nor demons
- Neither present nor future
- Nor any powers
- Neither height nor depth
- Nor (to make sure we've included everything!) anything else in all creation

. . . can separate us from the love of God.

Jesus is the Lord. All creation is under his lordship. He controls all those things that may threaten us.

Once you become absolutely persuaded of God's control over all things, then none of the things that tend to induce stress will harm you. Do you remember the list from the Holmes and

Rahe Social Readjustment Rating Scale outlined in chapter 2? We can paraphrase: not death, divorce, financial strain, changed work pressures nor anything else in all creation (or the forty-three life-change events) can separate you from the love of God in Christ Jesus. In him, you may rest secure.

Working it out

The best advice I can give you is: preach the above to yourself, and do so often.

Speaking to yourself may well be a sign of madness. However, I have already mentioned my belief that preaching to yourself is a sign of sanity. You might not want to verbalize these thoughts in public places, but refreshing your memory with these great truths throughout each day is essential. This will help you connect the truths of the gospel with the reality of living as a Christian in today's world. 'God is for me.' 'Nothing can separate me.' 'I am more than conqueror.' 'I am persuaded.' Pause and ponder.

I write this sensitively and cautiously, but I should warn you that God may well bring circumstances into your life in the near future to allow you to demonstrate that you do indeed believe this. I realize that God often seems to take us at our word when we ask him to teach us important truths from his Word, and it may well be that the circumstances he chooses to teach us these lessons might not be those that we would naturally choose.

The truths from Romans 8 are beautifully encapsulated in the hymn: 'How Firm a Foundation, Ye Saints of the Lord', believed to be written by Richard Keen in 1787:

> How firm a foundation, ye saints of the Lord,
> Is laid for your faith in His excellent Word!

What more can He say than to you He hath said
Who unto the Saviour for refuge have fled?

In ev'ry condition – in sickness, in health,
In poverty's vale or abounding in wealth,
At home or abroad, on the land or the sea –
As thy days may demand, so thy succour shall be.

'Fear not, I am with thee, oh, be not dismayed,
For I am thy God and will still give thee aid;
I'll strengthen thee, help thee, and cause thee to stand,
Upheld by My righteous, omnipotent hand.

'When through the deep waters I call thee to go,
The rivers of sorrow shall not overflow;
For I will be with thee thy troubles to bless
And sanctify to thee thy deepest distress.

'When through fiery trials thy pathway shall lie,
My grace, all-sufficient, shall be thy supply.
The flames shall not hurt thee; I only design
Thy dross to consume and thy gold to refine.

'The soul that on Jesus hath leaned for repose
I will not, I will not, desert to his foes;
That soul, though all hell should endeavour to shake,
I'll never, no never, no never, forsake!'

The world is looking for love. The search can manifest itself
in all kinds of ways and, for many, it is the driving force in
their life. But the big hope of Romans 8 is that men and
women will find their security and value in the Lord Jesus
Christ. I am convinced that the stresses and pressures of

modern living are put into proper perspective when we meditate on God's good and perfect plans for his children.

I have concluded this book by deliberating focusing on the deep theological truths of Romans 8. As I indicated at the beginning of the book, my primary interest in the topic of stress is theological, not medical, psychological or social. These final three chapters have shown that the best way to live the Christian life is by working out the practical implications of good Bible teaching.

Wouldn't it be great to regain control of your life? I more than suspect that the best help comes from beyond yourself. Hence, our special focus on considering God's loving intervention in this world to save us by sending his Son for us. Speaking personally, this is my deepest consolation when stress invades my life.

Conclusion: putting the pieces together

Sustaining the Christian life for the long haul

I do rather a lot of long-haul flying. I enjoy the privilege of seeing different parts of the world. But I do not enjoy the jet-lag and have found getting over it difficult.

The best advice for recovering from jet-lag seems to be as follows: before the flight, start doing everything you can to acclimatize yourself to your final destination. Eat according to the meal patterns of the country you are visiting, sleep according to their sleep patterns and set your clock in anticipation of the new time zone. That way, you are ready for your final destination before you arrive.

The same advice applies to sustaining the Christian life for the long haul. Our final destination is not this world, but rather our heavenly home. The best way to make the transition is to 'fix our eyes on things [and Jesus] above' and inculcate homesickness for heaven. Everything in this book has been written with this end in mind, to encourage living life in anticipation of eventually 'going home'. My hope is that by reading this book, you will be better sustained for the Christian life in the long haul. This will mean jettisoning the excess baggage which weighs us down.

Seven deadly sins

The so-called seven deadly sins have attracted the attention of famous authors, but in fact they were first listed in the Wisdom writings of the Bible. Proverbs 6:16–19 states, 'There are six things the Lord hateth, and seven that are an abomination unto Him' (kjv). Those seven things are:

1. a proud look
2. a lying tongue
3. hands that shed innocent blood
4. a heart that devises wicked plots
5. feet that are swift to run into mischief
6. a deceitful witness that uttereth lies
7. him that soweth discord among brethren.

I am sure that this list is not intended to be exhaustive, but these sins do resonate remarkably well with the challenges of living a Christian life in a world of stress.

Deadly sins contribute to stress

Pride (or vanity) is an excessive belief in our own abilities, something that interferes with our recognition of the grace of God. It has been called the sin from which all others arise. Pride drives me to project an image of control and independence to the world around me.

Envy is the desire for others' traits, statuses, abilities or situations. The media adds fuel to this dissatisfaction and encourages a consumerist outlook on life.

Gluttony is an inordinate desire to consume more than I require. Overeating and excessive social drinking are false quick-fixes for the problem of stress.

Lust is an inordinate craving for the pleasures of the body. Sensual stimulation is addictive and unsatisfying when it is not grounded in love.

Anger is manifested if I spurn love and opt instead for fury. It is often driven by having my wants spurned or challenged.

Greed (or covetousness) is the desire for material wealth or gain, ignoring the realm of the spiritual. Hedonism is the reigning religion in the Western world and can only be kept in check when my loves are turned back to God.

Sloth is the avoidance of physical or spiritual work. Stress makes me unfocused, distracted and unproductive.

Paul warns about the sins that come naturally from every human being. If you are not a Christian, these things may come naturally to you:

> [The acts of the flesh are obvious:] sexual immorality, impurity and debauchery; idolatry and witchcraft; hatred, discord, jealousy, fits of rage, selfish ambition, dissensions, factions and envy; drunkenness, orgies, and the like. I warn you, as I did before, that those who live like this will not inherit the kingdom of God.
> (Galatians 5:19–21)

By contrast, Paul lists the characteristics that should overflow from a Spirit-filled Christian:

> But the fruit of the Spirit is love, joy, peace, forbearance, kindness, goodness, faithfulness, gentleness and self-control.

Against such things there is no law. Those who belong to Christ Jesus have crucified the flesh with its passions and desires. Since we live by the Spirit, let us keep in step with the Spirit. Let us not become conceited, provoking and envying each other.
(Galatians 5:22–26)

We have noted that much of our stress is caused by seeking to be in control when total control just isn't possible. However, every Christian is rather like the demoniac who, after Jesus had ministered to him, was found 'sitting at Jesus' feet, dressed and in his right mind' (Luke 8:35). Control is found when we are back in harmony with our Creator.

This theme is picked up in the list of the fruit of the Spirit. Love comes first: through the Spirit, we learn to give as God gives, selflessly and generously. But through the same Spirit, we also gain self-control. The Spirit helps us to give of ourselves for the benefit of others, and so we find we are back in control of ourselves. Love is self-giving, which leads to self-control.

Remember, God is not stressed. And neither need we be when God is rightly enthroned in our lives.

Seven life-giving habits

1. Don't be overly impressed with your own importance.
2. Don't assume that everyone else has got it together.
3. Don't overeat: comfort food is not actually that comforting.
4. Make a covenant with your eyes not to lust, and remind yourself that sin might be sweet to the taste, but will turn sour in your stomach. A hard reality check on the damage caused by broken relationships will help.
5. Beware of the path from anger to sin and how easily you may slip down it.

6. Remember that you are already rich (at least relatively speaking).
7. Don't be lazy – even filling hours at the desk and frenetic activity can be a form of laziness if it involves merely frittering away time on trivia.

We might put these negative warnings in the form of positive statements:

1. You are valuable – at least, God seems to think so!
2. You should not expect perfection for yourself or others.
3. God has given us all things richly to enjoy.
4. Plan not to sin, and nip it in the bud.
5. Dissipate anger by focusing on God.
6. Enjoy what you have.
7. Put work in a broader context.

Summary of key lessons

This book has concentrated on some primary causes and effects of stress. We have considered the endemic nature of stress, recognizing that while stress is not an entirely new concept, it is certainly exacerbated by the pace, busyness and interconnectivity of modern living. We have considered how contact with the created world and good planning for leisure and worship (as well as work) is essential.

Primarily, though, this is a book about how biblical truths can help us view the world through the lens of our Creator God. By examining the Scriptures, we see how great God's love for us is in Christ Jesus. This should give us feelings of assurance, release from guilt, a disposition of joy and a settled conviction that God is more committed to his purposes than I ever can be. Ambition is brought into its right perspective, and anger is dissipated when I consider God's character. Moreover, it is tremendously liberating to realize that God wants me to be not just holy, but also happy.

Thomas, **Susan**, **Jack** and **Anna** – we all know people like them only too well. They are in our churches, our communities and in our families. We can use the deep truths from this book to challenge and encourage them to lift their eyes to greater horizons.

My hope is that this book will have helped individuals like Thomas, Susan, Jack and Anna – and you too – to begin a process of putting this life in the context of eternity. Remember the opening of this book: God is not stressed. And you will find great relief from stress when you reorder your life around God's good purposes for you. The end of the book is not the end of the process – it's only the beginning. My sincere hope is that I have outlined some principles of Christian living in such a way that they will sustain us all for the long haul.

Notes

1. Stress in perspective and lessons learned

1. Philip Yancey and Dr Paul Brands, *Pain: The Gift Nobody Wants* (Zondervan, 1993).
2. For example, Steve Covey, *Seven Habits of Highly Successful People* (Simon & Schuster, 1989, 2004).
3. There are several other personality indicators apart from the Myers-Briggs Type Indicator. Some claim that most American clergy are extroverts, while British clergy are introverts. For example, see http://johnmeunier.wordpress.com/2010/09/15/top-3-personality-types-for-clergy.

2. Assessing stress and remembering our Maker

1. See http://news.bbc.co.uk/1/hi/4695711.stm. Hoegaarden Beers commissioned this survey in 2005. It was published in many national newspapers, but is no longer available.
2. See www.rickmansworthherts.freeserve.co.uk/howard1.htm.
3. Thomas H. Holmes and Richard H. Rahe, 'The Social Readjustment Rating Scale', *Journal of Psychosomatic Research*,

11(2), August 1967, pp. 213–218, published by Elsevier Science Inc. All rights reserved.

4. See www.stress.org/holmes-rahe-stress-inventory.

5. There is an online version of this test at www.mindtools.com/pages/article/newTCS_82.htm.

6. www.bbc.co.uk/news/health-24756311.

7. www.billboard.com/articles/columns/chart-beat/1563850/amy-grant-chart-beat-meet-greet-video #GOTYSR2IAOdE3q8A.01.

3. Are Christians any less stressed than non-Christians?

1. An online version of this booklet may be found at www.simonvibert.com/writing/longingforparadise/index.htm.

2. www.huffingtonpost.com/2013/02/08/millennials-stress_n_2646947.html.

3. See Matthew 6:9–13.

4. See Henry Beveridge (ed.), *The Institutes of Religion* (Pacific Publishing Studio, 2011), Book One, where Calvin relates the Doctrine of the Knowledge of God with the Doctrine of the Knowledge of Ourselves.

4. The problem with the problem of stress

1. www.gallup.com/poll/142715/job-stress-workers-biggest-complaint.aspx.

2. Walter Bradford Cannon, *Bodily Changes in Pain, Hunger, Fear and Rage* (D. Appleton & Company, 1915).

3. Geoff Thompson, *Stress Buster* (Summersdale Publishers, 2005), p. 17.

4. If you are concerned that your stress might require some help from a medical doctor or is having more serious long-term effects, this website might help as a first port of call: www.mindandsoul.info.

5. Archibald Hart, *Adrenaline and Stress* (Thomas Nelson, 1995).

6. Elisabeth Wilson, *Stress-proof Your Life* (The Infinite Ideas Company, 2005, 2007), pp. 2, 39.

7. http://medical-dictionary.thefreedictionary.com/stress.

8. www.hse.gov.uk/stress/furtheradvice/whatisstress.htm.

9. Archibald Hart, *Adrenaline and Stress* (Thomas Nelson, 1995).

10. R. S. Lazarus and R. Launier, 'Stress-related transactions between person and environment', in L. A. Pervin and M. Lewis (eds.), *Perspectives in Interactional Psychology* (Plenum, 1978), p. 9. See also R. S. Lazarus and S. Folkman, *Stress, Appraisal and Coping* (Springer, 1974).

11. See www.nwlink.com/~donclark/hrd/history/arousal.html and www.dangreller.com/the-right-level-of-stimulus-yerkes-dodson-law for practical illustrations of how the research may be seen to work in practice.

5. Worry and refocusing

1. Corrie ten Boom, *Clippings from My Notebook* (Thomas Nelson Inc, 1982).

2. This is the way the Vulgate translated the Greek word *Makárioi* (Matthew 5:3).

3. D. H. Barlow, *Anxiety and Its Disorders* (Guilford Press, 1988), pp. 235–285.

4. One study in 2005 put the total medical cost for an individual diagnosed with any anxiety disorder in the US at $6,475 per year (equal to approximately £3,361 at the time); see 'The cost of treating anxiety: the medical and demographic correlates that impact total medical costs' in *Depression and Anxiety* (2005), 21(4), pp. 178–184. In the UK, the estimated cost of treating the 10 million sufferers of anxiety was put at £10 billion (£1,250 per person per year) in July 2013: see www.telegraph.co.uk/health/healthnews/10200562/Anxiety-disorders-cost-10-billion-a-year.html.

5. Laura D. Kubzansky, Ichiro Kawachi, Avron Spiro III, Scott T. Weiss, Pantel S. Vokonas and David Sparrow, *Is Worrying Bad for Your Heart? A Prospective Study of Worry and Coronary Heart Disease in the Normative Aging Study* (American Heart Association, 1997).

6. See http://resources.denisonforum.org/library/sermons/255.

7. Further helpful advice may be found in Will van der Hart and Rob Waller, *The Worry Book* (IVP, 2011).

8. For example, Elisabeth Wilson, *Stress-proof Your Life* (The Infinite Ideas Company, 2005, 2007).

9. Mary C. Crowley, *Be Somebody* (Crescendo Book Publications, 1974).

10. O. Hallesby, *Prayer* (Augsburg Publishing House, Minneapolis, and IVP, 1994). This book contains much wisdom on this topic.

11. There are many helpful tools on the market, but most useful to me has been David Allen's book *Getting Things Done* (Piatkus, 2001), which has lots of good advice. Not least is writing down 'next-action points' rather than lists, which enable you to know exactly what you next need to do when you stare at the long list of uncompleted tasks. I have also found that using a tool such as 'Evernote' enables me to synchronize notes, thoughts and lists across my smartphone, laptop and desktop computer (see https://evernote.com).

12. Robert McAfee Brown (ed.), *The Essential Reinhold Niebuhr: Selected Essays and Addresses* (Yale, 1986), p. 251.

6. Don't let the sun go down on your anger

1. Verbal comments made at a training session for church leaders at St Luke's Church, Wimbledon Park, 2001.

2. Dr Sandi Mann argues, '. . . on the one hand our expectations have risen steadily, and on the other hand, so have our stress levels . . . At the same time that we have become more

demanding as a nation, we are also living a more frenetic and frantic pace of life, which means our stress levels are raised.' See www.huffingtonpost.co.uk/sandi-mann/why-are-we-all-so-angry-these-days_b_2540474.html (accessed 24 January 2013).

3. www.scientificamerican.com/article.cfm?id=why-is-everyone-on-the-internet-so-angry.

4. The principal perpetrators were sent to jail for their abusive tweets.

5. See https://blog.twitter.com/en-gb/2013/our-commitment ?m=1.

6. Comments about God's character as being full of goodness, compassion, love, forgiveness and slowness to anger are repeated consistently throughout the Bible: Exodus 34:6; Numbers 14:18; Nehemiah 9:17; Psalms 86:15; 103:8; 145:8; Joel 2:13; Jonah 4:2; Nahum 1:3.

7. John T. Hower, 'Misunderstanding and mishandling of anger', *Journal of Psychology and Theology* (1974), 2(4), p. 272.

8. See J. I. Packer, *Knowing God* (IVP, 1973), p. 136.

9. Charles E. Cerling Jr, 'Anger: musings of a theologian/psychologist', *Journal of Psychology and Theology* (Winter 1974), 2(1), p. 13.

10. John E. Pedersen, 'A biblical view of anger', *Journal of Psychology and Theology* (Summer 1974), 2(3), p. 214.

11. Attributed to Aristotle.

12. LXX translation.

13. Cerling, 'Anger: musings of a theologian/psychologist', p. 14.

14. John Calvin, quoted in Cerling, p. 14.

15. Thomas Aquinas, *Summa Theologiae* 2, 158, ad 2.

16. Address at the Nelson Mandela Foundation in Houghton, Johannesburg, South Africa, 23 November 2004.

17. For more on this topic, see Gary Collins, *Christian Counselling, A Comprehensive Guide* (revised edition) (Word, Milton Keynes, 1989) – pp. 119–133 are particularly helpful.

18. See also Gary Collins, *Christian Counselling*, p. 125.

7. Be ambitious, but for the right reasons

1. See the Hoegaarden 2005 survey outlined in chapter 2.
2. I have written more about this in *Longing for Paradise*: www.simonvibert.com/writing/longingforparadise/index.htm.
3. http://pastormark.tv/2012/06/13/3-truths-about-the-church.
4. Several variations of this poem may be found on headstones around the world – for example, in 1857 in Balmoral Cemetery, Belfast: 'Stop traveller and cast an eye, As you are now so once was I. Prepare in time make no delay, For youth and time will pass away.'
5. www.omf.org/omf/us/resources__1/omf_archives/famous_china_inland_mission_quotations/c_t_studd.
6. Alister Chapman, *Godly Ambition. John Stott and the Evangelical Movement* (OUP, 2012), pp. 8–9.
7. Rick Warren, *The Purpose-driven Life* (Zondervan, 2002).

8. Work, rest and worship

1. See also Kevin DeYoung, *Crazy Busy: A (Mercifully) Short Book about a (Really) Big Problem* (Crossway, 2013).
2. Verna Wright, *The Lord's Day: A Medical Point of View* (Day One Publications, 2012).
3. *Frankston & Somerville Standard*, Saturday, 14 July 1934.
4. www.lordsday.co.uk/medical_point_of_view.htm.
5. A BBC article cites numerous examples of the use of this method of torture: http://news.bbc.co.uk/1/hi/3376951.stm.
6. www.truettcathy.com/about_recipe.asp (accessed 21 February 2014).
7. www.qideas.org/blog/wisdom-and-sabbath-rest.aspx.
8. *St. Augustine's Confessions* (Lib 1, 1–2, 2.5, 5: CSEL 33, 1–5).
9. http://e-n.org.uk/p-5428-The-Lord's-Day-a-medical-point-of-view.htm.

9. Joy and thankfulness as a way of life

1. See A. A. Milne's classic books *Winnie the Pooh* (1926) and *The House at Pooh Corner* (Methuen Co., 1928).

2. See John 3:16–21; Romans 1:18 – 2:16; Revelation 22:11–15.

3. See William G. Morrice, *Joy in the New Testament* (William B. Eerdmans, 1984), pp. 19–26: exultant joy (*agallian, aggalliasis*); optimism (*euthumein, euthumos*); gladness or good cheer (*euphrainein, euphrosunē*); pleasure (*hēdone, hēdus, hēdēos*); courage (*tharsein, tharrein, tharsos*); hilarity (*hilaros, hilarotēs*); boasting (*kauchasthai, kauchēma, kauchēsis*); blessedness or happiness (*makarios, makarizein, makarismos*); leaping for joy (*skirtan*); inward joy (*chairein, chara*); shared joy (*sunchairein*).

4. D. Martyn Lloyd-Jones, *Christian Depression* (Pickering, 1981), pp. 112–113.

5. *The Works of Jonathan Edwards* (Vol. 2) (Banner of Truth, 1997 [1834]), p. 20.

6. J. I. Packer, *Laid-back Religion* (IVP, 1987), p. 95.

7. See further Philippians 1:4; 1:18; 2:2; 3:1.

8. See also Romans 14:17; Galatians 5:22–23.

9. Morrice, *Joy in the New Testament*, p. 129, quoting C. von Weizsäcker.

10. There will be more to say on this important verse in chapter 11.

11. John Piper, *Desiring God: Meditations of a Christian Hedonist* (IVP, 1986), pp. 72–73.

12. John Piper, *Desiring God*.

10. Relax, you are pre-approved

1. 'Once the element of competition has gone, pride has gone.' C. S. Lewis, *Mere Christianity* (HarperOne, 1952), p. 122.

2. Roy Jenkins, *Churchill: A Biography* (Pan Books, 2001).

3. See *A Commentary on St Paul's Epistle to the Galatians* (Zondervan, 1939 [1539]), comment on Galatians 3:13.

4. Martin Luther, *Commentary on Romans* (trans. J. Theodore

Mueller) (Kregel Publications, 2003); see comment on
Romans 1:17.

5. For example, Ephesians 5:21 – 6:4.

11. Let God be King

1. See www.poemhunter.com/poem/invictus.
2. I am grateful to John Dixon's book, *If I Were God I'd End All the Pain* (Matthias Media, 2003), for this insight.
3. Ephesians 1:11 teaches something very similar: 'In him we were also chosen, having been predestined according to the plan of him who works out everything in conformity with the purpose of his will . . .'
4. J. I. Packer, *Evangelism and the Sovereignty of God* (IVP, 1961), p. 17.
5. Alleged to have been found on a CSA casualty at the Devil's Den, Gettysburg.
6. www.ruthvdb.com, 'On Attitudes', posted on 25 July 2013, reproduced with Ruth's permission.

12. Remember that God is for you!

1. David Dooley (ed.), *The Collected Works of G.K. Chesterton: Vol. One* (Ignatius, San Francisco, 1986).
2. God's wrath is justly revealed (Romans 1:18–19); in Romans chapter 2, Paul explores how a just judge can remain just and acquit the guilty; in 3:21–31, he explains how God may righteously judge sin and yet, at the same time, spare sinful people, by providing in Christ a 'sacrifice of atonement' (v. 25).
3. Appeared in *Slave Songs of the United States* (1867) as part of a collection of traditional American songs.
4. The word is *thlipsis*, meaning 'to squeeze, pressurize'. We could translate it along a range, from stress to outright hostility.

5. Timothy Keller, *Walking with God through Pain and Suffering* (Hodder & Stoughton, 2013), p. 304.
6. W. Martin, 'Expository Times, 1972–73', p. 276. Quoted in Leon Morris, *The Epistle to the Romans* (IVP, 1988), p. 340.
7. J. McKenzie, 'Expository Times, 1959–60', p. 319. Quoted in Leon Morris, *The Epistle to the Romans* (IVP, 1988), p. 340.

Also by Simon Vibert

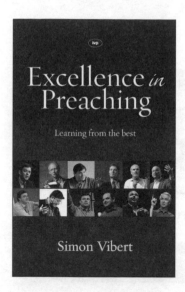

Excellence in Preaching
Learning from the best
Simon Vibert

ISBN: 978-1-84474-519-7
176 pages, paperback

What makes some preaching gripping – unforgettable even?
What can we learn from the best preachers?
How can we appreciate great preaching, often at the click of a
mouse, without devaluing the role of the local church minister?

'Without creating a guru mentality, I focus on one positive
aspect from each preacher and offer ideas on how other
preachers might emulate them,' says author Simon Vibert.
He also looks at the Bible's own take on good preaching, and
focuses on the exemplary models of Jesus and Paul.

This is not a how-to manual, nor a biblical theology of
preaching, nor even a critique of the subjects. Rather, it is a
focus on modern-day practitioners, from whom all preachers
can form a composite picture of excellence, and from whom all
preachers would do well to learn.

*'An inspiring, accessible and engaging book for preachers, at
whatever stage in their preaching ministry ... A must-read for
anyone who takes preaching seriously.'* Revd Clare Hendry

Available from your local Christian bookshop or **www.thinkivp.com**

For more information about IVP
and our publications visit

www.ivpbooks.com

Get regular updates at **ivpbooks.com/signup**
Find us on **facebook.com/ivpbooks**
Follow us on **twitter.com/ivpbookcentre**

Inter-Varsity Press, a company limited by guarantee registered in England and Wales, number 05202650. Registered office IVP Bookcentre, Norton Street, Nottingham NG7 3HR, United Kingdom. Registered charity number 1105757.